HISTORY

OF THE

OLD GREYFRIARS' CHURCH
EDINBURGH

OLD GREYFRIARS' CHURCH—East Gable.

HISTORY
OF THE
OLD GREYFRIARS'
CHURCH
EDINBURGH

BY

WILLIAM MOIR BRYCE

WITH CHAPTER ON THE
SUBSCRIBING OF THE NATIONAL COVENANT
By D. HAY FLEMING, LL.D.

EDINBURGH AND LONDON
WILLIAM GREEN AND SONS
1912

PREFACE

THE Church of the Greyfriars—now known as Old Grey-friars—of Edinburgh, was founded three hundred years ago, and the following History of the famous old building has been compiled at the instigation of my friend and pastor, the Rev. A. B. Grant, B.D., the present incumbent. The recent discovery of an early portion of Wariston's Diary has upset the conventional story of the subscribing of the National Covenant, and, in the circumstances, I appealed to my learned friend, Dr. Hay Fleming, the discoverer of that manuscript, to undertake the writing of a special chapter on a subject on which he is a recognised authority. The result of his research and study will be found under Chapter VIII., and I have to tender him my grateful thanks for all his kind labours. My thanks are also due to Mr. John Cameron Robbie, my professional assistant, for much kind assistance ungrudgingly bestowed; and, lastly, to Dr. King Hewison for his kind permission in allowing the prints of Alexander Henderson and George Gillespie to appear.

WILLIAM MOIR BRYCE.

EDINBURGH, 11 BLACKFORD ROAD,
    1st March 1912.

v

TABLE OF CONTENTS

ILLUSTRATIONS

Photogravure of Alexander Henderson, by Messrs. T. & R. Annan & Sons, Glasgow.

Collotypes by The Zinco Collotype Co., M'Donald Road, Edinburgh.

Zincographic Plates ⎱ *by Messrs. Bell, Fowler, & Co. Ltd., York Place,*
Photographs ⎰ *Edinburgh.*

ALEXANDER HENDERSON

From a painting in possession of the Marquis of Tweeddale

HISTORY

OF THE

OLD GREYFRIARS' CHURCH

OF

EDINBURGH

———◆———

THE Parish Church of the Greyfriars of Edinburgh, now known as the Old Greyfriars, is a squat, ugly building, with no pretension to architectural style or beauty. It was erected by the Town Council of Edinburgh three hundred years ago, and forms a fair example of the debased taste that prevailed in those days. The usual tower was placed at the west end; while the apex of the eastern wall was "adorned" by a pediment. Both have since disappeared under the destructive effects of gunpowder and fire; but, with these exceptions, the building still presents, externally, much the same general features as when first erected. Despite, however, all its architectural defects, the Church of the Greyfriars occupies a prominent and honourable position in the annals of the Church of Scotland. Within its rough rubble walls the National Covenant—that epoch-making document which has left its indelible marks on Scottish life and character—

A

had its birth; and in the graveyard without, repose the ashes of many of the heroes and martyrs who suffered in its defence during the Episcopalian ascendancy. There, also, in the fulness of time, their fierce and brutal persecutors found a last resting-place; and now both persecutor and victim sleep peacefully together under the same sod. It was also in the large field lying to the south, and at that time known as the Inner or South Greyfriar Yard, that the unfortunate Covenanting prisoners captured at Bothwell Bridge in 1679 were interned and kept without shelter of any kind, and almost without food or water, for a period of nearly five months. Under the stern hand of persecution, Presbyterianism became to a large extent racialised; and, towards this end, the long line of eminently capable, and in many cases even brilliant, ministers who occupied the Greyfriars' pulpit have largely contributed. It was one of their number who inaugurated, during the lifetime of the present generation, the reformation in the mode of conducting public worship that has since been adopted by all our leading Presbyterian bodies. Under the enthusiasm and fervour of the Covenanting period, the forms of divine service introduced in 1564 by John Knox gradually became obsolete, as formal, and thereby savouring of Popery or Prelacy; and it was their re-introduction along with certain other improvements suitable to the present age, by the late Dr. Robert Lee of Old Greyfriars, that has been the direct means of restoring our ancient and historic Church of Scotland to its true position in the country.

With such a record, it is, perhaps, not amiss that at a time when the Old Greyfriars' Church celebrates its tercentenary, the history of the church and its graveyard should be compiled. Modern historical criticism demands exactitude founded on contemporary and original evidence; and it will be observed that, in several instances, old traditions have had to be swept away and replaced by fact. Now, at the western end of the church, another was added in course of time, and the two thenceforth became respectively known as the Old and the New Greyfriars. The sites of these two churches as well as that of the graveyard itself—excluding the western and southern extensions—formed the demesne of a colony of Grey Friars of Observance ; and it is with a brief account of these friars that our story naturally begins.

I

THE GREY FRIARS

The Grey Friars made their first appearance in Scotland in the year 1231. Their founder was the gentle St. Francis of Assisi, who became in the early years of the thirteenth century one of the greatest personages of his day. When lying on a bed of sickness, his heart became filled to overflowing with the thought of the miseries and sufferings of the poor. The Church had viewed her obligations towards the poor with ever-increasing neglect, until her salaried servants had become almost complete strangers to practical Christianity. Religion had become synonymous with the mere formal celebration of the divine offices, and had no more than a haphazard relation with suffering humanity. St. Francis— surely one of the saintliest in the whole calendar of the Roman hagiology—resolved to devote his life to the moral and spiritual regeneration of the poor ; and, the better to accomplish his purpose, he adopted the badge of humble poverty for himself and his followers. In his own poetical language he espoused the Lady Poverty, and from this union sprang the Franciscan Order and the union of Charity and

Religion which brought anew the soothing influence of Christianity into the lives of the poor, the outcast, and the leper.   He called his followers friars—*frères*, the brothers of mankind—and to the general body he gave the name of the Order of Friars Minor—*i.e.* the lesser or humbler Order. In later times, from the colour of their dress, they were generally spoken of in this country as the Grey Friars. Their habit, which they wore even when threadbare and patched, consisted of a long tunic with a hood made of undyed wool, and bound round the waist by a cordelière or cord ; but in winter they were provided with a cloak of the same rough material.   Their feet were bare, although in our country they used sandals in rough weather.   In the early days of the movement the friars slept in the porches of churches, or built for themselves a rough shelter of sticks, mud, and straw.   The Rule of Poverty imposed upon his followers by the Poverello, as he was loved to be designated in his own country, was severe.   " I firmly command all the friars," he said, " not to accept coin or money in any manner of way either by their own hands or through an interposed person," and to " appropriate nothing to themselves, neither house nor place nor anything.   As pilgrims and strangers in the world, let them seek alms with confidence, and they need feel no shame in doing so, because the Lord made Himself poor in this world for us." [1]   Mendicancy was, of course, the natural corollary to the profession of poverty ; but, visionary though he was, he also chose the exercise of manual labour as the most certain antidote to apathy among his brethren. In short, he elevated work to the rank of a Christian duty : " Let those friars to whom the Lord has given the grace of working, labour faithfully and devoutly in such wise that, while they abolish idleness—the enemy of the soul—they do not extinguish the spirit of holy prayer and devotion, to

[1] For authorities, etc., see my work on *The Scottish Grey Friars*, published in 1909.

which all temporal matters should be subservient. Let them receive, as the reward of their labour, the necessaries of life, but neither coin nor money, and that humbly, as becomes the servants of God and the followers of most holy poverty." Most of the friars at this date were laymen taken from their ordinary outdoor avocations, and the lay element continued down to the time of the Reformation to be largely represented in the Franciscan community. Looking to the then accepted ideas of a religious Order, this precept was scarcely less revolutionary than that which enjoined a life of poverty, and, towards the end of his life, we find it emphasised in his Testament : " I was wont to labour with my hands, and I wish still to labour, and I earnestly desire that every friar may work at some honest task. And as for those who do not know how, let them learn to work, not from a desire to receive the price of their labour, but to show a good example, and to eschew idleness." Sufficient, perhaps, has been said to illustrate the Franciscan rule of life, and it only remains to add that St. Francis possessed in an eminent degree that courteous charm of manner which subsequently became the standard of imitation not only among his own friars, but among all the clergy of the Church of Rome.

Armed with the authority of the Holy See, the Franciscan propaganda evoked the greatest enthusiasm among all classes of the community, and the ranks of the friars in the course of a few years became swelled by thousands of recruits taken from every grade of society. The death of St. Francis in 1226 brought about two distinct changes in the constitution of the Order. The Poverello was a layman and unlearned ; but his successors recognised that, in their position as public preachers and confessors, education had become a necessity. Friary schools for novices were established, and friar students were to be seen at the University of Paris and other *studia generalia*. It was an age of emotional enthusiasm, and the desire for learning became so intense that in a short time there arose from within their ranks many of the most distinguished scholars in Europe. In consequence, there was a large increase of the clerical element within the Order. Then, the Rule of Poverty laid down by St. Francis became the subject of internecine contention. The difficulty of maintaining a whole race of friars on the proceeds of begging aided by casual labour had become felt, and many of the friars in dire distress had been forced to accept gifts of money, etc., from the devout. Dissension arose, and, ultimately, after centuries of bitter controversy, the whole Order became split into two sections. Those who accepted gifts were formed into one body, and became known as the Conventual Grey Friars ; while to the remainder, who attempted to carry out in all its severity the injunctions of St. Francis, was given the name of the Grey Friars of Observance. The two divisions separated, each under its own Minister-General ; but, ultimately, the Papacy gave to the Friars of Observance the senior position, and appointed their General as the head of the whole Order, the superior of the Conventuals being termed their Master-General.

II

THE CONVENTUAL GREY FRIARS

Scotland was unfavourably situated for the successful exercise of the Franciscan ideal. As a country it was sterile, bleak, and cold; while the general body of the people were steeped in poverty. A spirit of unrest—what the Franciscan historian calls the *motus turbulenti*—prevailed, and the country was constantly ravaged by war, either through internecine feuds, or with our "auld enemies of England." Nevertheless, the friars who settled in Berwick in 1231 succeeded, in course of time, in establishing six other friaries in this country—in Roxburgh, Haddington, Dundee, Lanark, Dumfries, and Kirkcudbright. During the wars with England several of these friaries were burned and destroyed; while the Warden of that at Dumfries was carried off in 1548 as a hostage to Carlisle, and there cruelly hanged by Lord Wharton. It is not surprising that these friars, when forced by want, should have transgressed their Rule, and accepted small monetary gifts from their local friends and sympathisers. From the returns furnished after the Reformation to the Lord Treasurer, we learn that the annual rentals belonging to these six friaries amounted altogether to a sum of only two hundred pounds Scots— equal in sterling money to £16, 13s. 4d.—and we may easily forgive this small transgression of their Rule of Poverty. The Franciscan ideals were lofty, and transcended those of all the other religious communities; but life under their Rule of Poverty was a physical impossibility. The acceptance of monetary gifts, however small, placed these six friaries within the category of the Conventuals.

III

THE EDINBURGH GREY FRIARS OF OBSERVANCE

It was not until the middle of the fifteenth century that the Grey Friars of Observance made their appearance in this country. In response, it is alleged, to an invitation made by King James I. during his lifetime, a mission consisting of six friars, one of whom was a Scot, under the leadership of a learned Dutchman, Father Cornelius of Zierikzee, came from the Low Countries and settled in Edinburgh. In anticipation of their arrival a number of the citizens, headed by James Douglas of Cassellis, had erected a friary in a " conspicuous and conveniently situated portion of that metropolitan city." The Franciscan chronicler, who wrote in 1586, tells us that the friary buildings seemed " not to be the dwellings of poor men but of the great ones," and that Cornelius refused to accept the town's gift, because St. Francis had ordered the friars to dwell in poor and neglected houses. Eight years later, this " despiser of the world " yielded to the representations of the Bishop of St. Andrews, and accepted them " as pilgrims according to their Rule." The Observance was still in its infancy, and these protestations against the acceptance of plain stone buildings were at this time common occurrences in every country.

The site selected for the friary was a plot of land which, in modern topography, is bounded on the north by the Grassmarket and by the Candlemaker Row on the east. The angle formed by these streets is now covered by buildings ; but in those days there were only two tenements, " back and fore," on the eastern side. The plan on page 154 shows the position of the buildings and the friary yards, with this explanation, that the southern portion of the present graveyard described as the " Croft " or the " Uppermost Yard " was not acquired by the friars until a century later. The gateway was near the entrance to the Grassmarket, and the present northern doorway was not erected until the year 1562, when the friary with its yards fell into the hands of the city. The portion facing the Grassmarket round the corner to the two tenements previously referred to was gradually feued off ; while to the south-east of these tenements another building was erected. The whole of the ground formed the north-eastern flank of the lands of Highriggs, which extended from the Grassmarket southward to the Burgh Loch, and were bounded on the east by the "Loaning," or Candlemaker Row as it is now termed, and on the west by the Westport, at that time known as the road leading from the West Bow to the Tollcross. These lands had been, from the year 1388, in the possession of the well-known Edinburgh family of Tours of Inverleith. In the year 1479 the friars were confirmed in their rights to the ground by a formal charter granted by James III. under the Great Seal.

Returning to the infancy of the Observance in Edinburgh, the chronicler speaks of the rapidity with which the " fame of Cornelius and his associates spread in every direction," and that numbers of learned Scots found their way thither from the universities of Paris, Cologne, and elsewhere, begging for admission into the ranks of the " Poor of Christ." The arrival of the Dutch friars was, undoubtedly, an event of no ordinary importance in the annals of reformation within the then Scottish Church. Like the first Franciscans, these revivalists quickened the pulse of religious life, which was fast relapsing into the passive state from which it had been rescued by St. Francis. From this centre the friars were enabled, under the *ægis* of King James II. and his two successors, to establish friaries in several other of the important burghs ; and it was through the intercession of his Queen, Mary of Gueldres, that Pope Pius II. sanctioned by Bull, dated 9th June 1463,[1] and known as the *Intelleximus te*, the erection of three or four Observant friaries in this country, including that at Edinburgh. Queen Mary was personally of a delicate constitution, and had no fewer than three medical attendants. One of these was a foreigner whom she probably brought with her to this country in 1449 ; while another was a distinguished Scot of the name of Crannok, who became a friar. In the Exchequer Rolls for

[1] The late Bishop Dowden accepted this date as that of the first appearance in Edinburgh of the Observatines ; but this is clearly a mistake.

B

the year 1461 there is a notice of a payment of £20 Scots to Friar Crannok as medicinar or physician to the Queen, and in the following year this friar was elected Warden of the friary in succession to Father Cornelius, who then returned to his native land. The appointment of a physician to the wardenship naturally recalls the fact that the Grey Friars, from their extensive experience among the poor, made medicine a special study ; and that they were the first in Europe to place it on a scientific basis. In 1461 the friars received the first instalment of £50 as part of a sum of £150 allocated by James II. during his lifetime, for the reparation of their friary. The money was advanced to the King by Nicolas Spethy, who, as royal money-lender, may be considered the prototype of George Heriot.

Of the personal life and work of these friars but little is known, and, indeed, their activity among the sick and the poor is probably the most obscure chapter of their history. Then, as at the present day, the picturesque charity of the gentle Poverello had become subordinated to the fetish of theology and the minutely ordered life of the Churchman. Poverty among the masses, however, was a problem of ever-increasing gravity, with which the limited resources of the friary could scarcely hope to grapple. The friars must, therefore, be regarded more as workers among the poor than as their munificent benefactors. For this rôle they were pre-eminently fitted by their severe training in the school of self-denial, and, whatever their degree of enthusiasm may have been, their contemporaries were not slow to recognise them as the " friends " or " fathers of the poor." The friary became a centre to which a large section of the hungry poor looked for food which the friars managed to procure for them. In this respect, the friars became the recognised assistants of the chaplains of St. Giles in the distribution of obituary doles among the poor—in these days a fashionable form of charity among the wealthy burghers and clergymen in Edinburgh. Heritable securities were bequeathed for the celebration after death of anniversary services at some altar in St. Giles, and with the view of enhancing these occasions by deeds of piety, certain doles or " portions " of meat and drink were ordered to be handed over to specified institutions for division among their poor. The composition of the " portions " varied according to the whim of the testator. In some cases it consisted of " three pennies in bread, three in beer, and also three pennies in flesh, fish, cheese, or butter as the season[1] requires "; while, in others, it consisted of a loaf of white bread worth fourpence, and sixpence in money placed on the top—" upon the heid of ilk." The number of the portions differed in the respective Charters of Mortification; but a large number were invariably entrusted to the Observatine[2] Friars of Edinburgh. As auxiliaries of the parochial clergy of St. Giles the friars regularly preached in the public streets of the city, and, in return, they received from the Magistrates an annual " pensioun " of six barrels of sowens beer—a beverage consisting of sour beer mixed with the fluff or refuse of oatmeal, and much relished by the labouring classes. In 1464, during the wardenship of Friar Crannok, the friars were accorded permission by the Provost of St. Giles to " war for God in the Church or Chapel of St. John the Baptist belonging to my church, outwith the burgh of Edinburgh." This chapel may, as hinted in an entry in the Register of the Great Seal, have been situated on the west side of the West Bow—at that time a mere track—but the exact site, the period during which it was occupied, and its fate when abandoned by the friars are all unknown. The cordiality of the Provost's letter—which was confirmed by the diocesan of the district, Bishop Kennedy of St. Andrews—marks the change

---

[1] Flesh and fish were scarce commodities during winter.

[2] The word Observatine was used by a Scottish historian two hundred years ago, and has been adopted as more euphonious than that of Observantine.

that had taken place by this time in the attitude of the parochial clergy towards the friars. Now the laity had been thirled for centuries to the ministrations of the clergy of the parish in which they resided, and the latter stoutly resented any interference with their vested rights and monetary privileges. The struggle between the friars and the Churchmen was long and bitter ; but, supported by the Curia, the Grey Friars emerged the most highly centralised corporation within the Church. Their Charter of Liberties—the *Super Cathedram*, 18th February 1300 of Boniface VIII.—secured all but complete personal liberty to the layman in the exercise of his religion ; and it has remained *mutatis mutandis* the most conspicuous landmark in the democratic character of our own Church at the present day. Thereunder, the devout observer of religious duties enjoyed full liberty in the selection of the laver of his conscience. Confident in the absolution granted by the friar priest, the parishioner could demand the sacraments ; while attendance at a Mass either in the parish or friary church discharged his obligation on

A GREY FRIAR PREACHING.
14th Century MS.

the Sabbath morning and feast days. On death-bed, the last offices of the Church were received from his chosen celebrant, priest or friar, and the cemetery of the friary or the parish was his last resting-place according to a deliberate choice made when in life. His goods and gear alone perpetuated the distinction between the voluntary and the official clergy. The latter retained the right to join him in wedlock, to baptize his child, and to claim his tithes and deplete his succession under the guise of mortuary dues.

The victory was entirely the work of the Conventual Grey Friars, who, from want of support, had, as we have seen, failed to reach the Franciscan ideal of personal asceticism; but their Observatine brethren were now at hand to stir the piety of the country to its depths. Of the immense popularity of the latter with all classes, from the King on the throne to the peasant in the fields, there can be no shadow of doubt. As public preachers they competed with their friends the Black Friars; while in the hearing of confession they possessed the confidence of the whole community. Their advice and admonitions were disinterested, as they

THE GREY FRIARS, IN IMITATION OF THE
APOSTLES, RECEIVING THE CROWN OF
THE ELECT.
14th Century MS.

accepted no recompense either for themselves individually, or for their friary. The friary church was in the eyes of the people the most sacred spot on earth, and, hence, burial within its precincts was considered a certain road to heaven. The beautiful Church of the Ara Cœli at Rome—the general headquarters of the Observatines—and the other friary churches at Florence, Venice, and many other places, are thickly strewn with monuments erected by the leading people in their respective districts; but our knowledge regarding the friary at Edinburgh in this respect is a blank. The records kept by the friars were few in number, and of these none have survived the storm of the Reformation. Then, as the brethren were forbidden to take any share either in public or private affairs, their existence even is hardly ever referred to in any of our native histories. Certainly, all our local historians make the assertion that Mary of Gueldres was, on her arrival in Edinburgh in 1449, taken to this Grey Friary, and that the unfortunate Henry VI. of England, when driven furth of his own country, also sought and obtained shelter there. Both statements are erroneous; it was at the Priory of the Black Friars that both were hospitably lodged. Tytler also, when relating the story of the picturesque betrothal by proxy of the infant children of James III. and Henry VII. of England, identifies the lower chamber of the Grey Friary as the scene of this incident; whereas it was at the guest-house attached to the Priory of the Black Friars that the espousals were held. In their personal life the Edinburgh friars do not seem to have suffered from the hardships that overtook their Conventual brethren. Their chronicler informs us that of the three modes allowed to them of providing for their own sustenance — offerings, begging, and manual labour—the offerings came in such abundance that they rarely had occasion to resort to either begging or manual labour in order to procure the necessaries of life. He asserts that, " even in the last days when Religion was tottering to its fall," the daily alms of the "King, the princes, bishops, lords, and people of the realm" were offered in such profusion that the Warden found it necessary to return a large number of the gifts to the donors.   The sovereigns of Scotland were undoubtedly the staunchest and most generous supporters of the Edinburgh Grey Friars.   From the Exchequer Rolls we gather that they received from the Lord Chamberlain weekly doles in "eatables and drinkables" of fourteen loaves of bread, beer, and kitchen provisions to the value of ten shillings.   This allowance seems to have been afterwards altered into an annual grant of one chalder of wheat and another of barley.   Casual charities were also received as tokens of the royal favour;   and during the plague of 1505 a boll of wheat was sent to them by the Chamberlain.   In the early years of the sixteenth century the friars seem to have developed a taste for the unclean but savoury pig.   In 1518 the Royal Comptroller paid for a mart—a carcass of a pig—and one pig bestowed on them as alms of the King, and in 1532 for four Orkney marts; while four years later the royal charities consisted of six marts and four pigs from Orkney, six other carcasses of pigs, and two skins.   In 1538 the Comptroller paid £9 for certain marts and pigs delivered to the friars.   After the year 1546, the friars were paid annually the sum of £20 in lieu of the marts and pigs.   From the royal privy purse occasional sums of from 20s. to 42s. were also handed over to the friars by the Lord Treasurer.   As previously mentioned, the municipal charities consisted of the annual payment of six barrels of sowens beer; while from the great Incorporation of Hammermen the friars received annually the sum of 20s.   Only four testaments with bequests in favour of the friars are known, and these, with the exception of that of Gavin Dunbar, Archbishop of Glasgow—£6, 13s. 4d.—are all of trifling value.   Their chronicler states that there were always fifty to sixty friars in residence.

THE LETTER T, WHICH ST. FRANCIS, FROM ITS RESEMBLANCE TO THE CROSS, LOVED TO APPEND TO HIS LETTERS.

he friars found their strongest supporter and greatest benefactor in King James IV. He built for them a friary in Stirling at his own expense, and he constituted the Warden, Friar Ranny, his confessor. It was in consequence of the admonitions of this friar that he placed round his waist the famous iron belt, as a penance for his share in the rebellion which terminated in the murder of the King, his father. The belt was lined with worsted to prevent it chafing the skin. During his short reign, the country experienced a marked advance in material prosperity ; and, perhaps, Edinburgh never looked gayer or brighter than upon that sunny morning in August 1503, when his bride, the Princess Margaret of England, made her State entry into the city seated behind the chivalrous King James on a palfrey of honour. The principal highway from the south at that time was known as the " Loaning," and afterwards as the Grey Friars' or Bristo Port ; and here, says the English herald, " Ther war many honest people of the Town and of the Countre aboute, honestly arrayed, all on horsebak, and so, by Ordre, the King and the Qwene entred within the said Towne. At the entrynge of that same cam in Processyon the Grey Freres, with the Crosse and sum Relicks, the which was presented by the Warden to the Kynge for to kysse, bot he wold not before the Qwene ; and he had hys Hed barre during the ceremonies." The story of the " Fyancells " as narrated by the herald is exceedingly quaint and interesting. Professionally a man of pageantry, he revels in the minutest details of the various ceremonies he witnessed ; and he has given us the most vivid portraiture that real history has preserved of Edinburgh and its citizens as they appeared four centuries ago. It was a strange coincidence that the Princess should come to Scotland under the charge of the Earl of Surrey, who, ten years later, commanded the English army on the unhappy field of Flodden ; and we are told that the youthful monarch displayed much friendship towards his martial visitor. Among the slain were Sir Alexander Lauder of Blyth, then Provost of Edinburgh, and his four bailies. Sir Alexander must have had some premonition of personal disaster. On 17th August 1513, two days before the unfortunate Provost, accompanied by his bailies and contingent of Edinburgh burghers, joined the Scottish army on the Burgh Muir, he obtained Crown confirmation of his Charter of Mortification, in which he provided, in the event of his death, for the celebration of anniversary services in St. Giles. Being a man of considerable wealth, he also made provision for the issue of sixty " portions "—each of the value of ninepence, and consisting of bread, beer, and fish, or flesh—and of these the Grey Friars received twelve for division among their poor. King James had taken the Observatines under his special care,

GREY FRIARS CHANTING THE OFFICE.
14th Century MS.

C

and appointed himself their Royal Protector; and in the MS. Obituary Register belonging to the friars of Aberdeen— the sole example of its kind now extant—we learn that anniversary services on his behalf were regularly held. It is certain that similar services would be celebrated in all the Observatine friaries, including that at Edinburgh. One immediate result of the battle was the erection by the citizens of the defensive wall, now known as the Flodden Wall, round the southern side of the city. To save both time and expense, the Magistrates ordained that all the " heid dykis " and all other walls on the chosen route should be built up " weill and competently of heicht and thiknes as efferis," and incorporated in the Wall; so that " the towne be fermly closit about, swa at thair be na entres bot at the ports of the samyn." In this way the whole of the southern and western boundary walls of the friary were, during the years 1513 to 1515, strengthened and heightened so as to complete the line and become part of the Flodden Wall.[1] The friary walls were further defended by a tower or blockhouse which must have been situated at the salient angle at the southwest corner of the present graveyard; and from the City Records we learn that the Magistrates issued special instructions on 30th April 1578 to platform " the blekhouse at the Blakfreris and the Greyfreris, the Freir Port and West Port." Our local historians, following the vague statement in Maitland's *History*, believed that the Flodden Wall passed through the graveyard until it joined Bristo Port, and Kincaid professed to identify certain traces of the wall. These, however, were the remains of what was called the mid-dyke dividing the Croft or Uppermost Yard from the northern portion of the friary ground. This Croft or yard must have been held at first by the friars under a lease, and was devoted by them to pastoral uses. The Comp-

---

[1] For the complete story of the Flodden Wall, see my article in *Book of the Old Edinburgh Club*, vol. ii. p. 61.

troller narrates in the Exchequer Rolls that in 1527 they were paid the sum of £11, 8s. for " six barrels of suet " sold to the King. Ultimately the Croft was purchased on 24th February 1540–41, by the notorious Cardinal Betoun on behalf of the friars for a sum of £20.[1] The Cardinal seems to have been favourably disposed towards the Edinburgh friars, and in the Rental of the Archbishopric there appear, between the years 1539–43, four payments by him in alms amounting altogether to £26, 13s. 4d.; while, even after his murder at the hands of Norman Leslie and his associates, they received on his behalf two bolls of corn and four of barley from the tithes of the church at Kirkliston. We also find that when Friar Ludovic Williamson, the Provincial Minister of the Observatines, and other four friars attended the meeting of the Chapter General held at Mantua in 1541, the Cardinal contributed £11 towards their expenses. On their way thither, the friars passed through England under the protection of a safe-conduct from Henry viii.

The results of the disaster at Flodden were immediate and of long endurance. The nascent prosperity of the country was checked, and the bonds of discipline in both Church and State loosened. The country became exposed to the selfish machinations of an ambitious, turbulent, and unscrupulous nobility; while a spirit of decadence in both morals and religion was quickly manifested among the general body of the beneficed clergy, who neglected the pastoral duties of their office. In this *impasse*, the friars —both Grey and Black—became their willing substitutes; and, in the course of a few years, they were to be seen everywhere preaching in the cathedrals and parish churches, and administering the services of the Church to the great satisfaction of the people. The cherished hopes of St. Francis that his friars would become the auxiliaries of the parochial

---

[1] " *In viginti libris liberatis fratribus Minoribus de Edinburgh ad emendam croftam adjacentem corum orto.*"—*MS. Rental, Archbish. St. Andrews*, Adv. Lib.

clergy were now more than realised. The gradual circula-
tion of the Lutheran doctrines throughout the country made
no alteration in the debased lives of the clergy ; and, during
the whole period of the evolution of the Reformation, the
friars became, in effect, the sole professors of the art of
preaching. Henryson furnishes an example of the manner in
which the Grey Friars garnished their sermons with illustra-
tions from the Old and New Testaments, or the lives of the
Saints, as well as by fables, pithy stories, apophthegms, and
legends :—

> " Adew, my friend ; and gif that ony speiris
> Of this Fable, sa schortly I conclude,
> Say thow I left the laif unto the Freris
> To mak exempill and ane similitude."

A singular entry in the prosaic records of the Lord Treasurer
illustrates the privilege enjoyed by a friar confessor when
Scotland was still a daughter of Rome. In this instance,
an Observatine of Edinburgh learned from a penitent thief
that 63 ounces of the King's silver plate had been stolen
and " placed in wed "—pawned—for the sum of £20. This
information was communicated to the officials of the Court,
and in due course the money was handed over to the friars
as intermediaries in the process of restitution, the name of
neither thief nor resetter being divulged : " Item, delivirit
to the Gray Friars for 63 unce silver stollin fra the King, and
revelit to thaim in confessioune, be the Kingis precept, to
the men that had the silver werk in wed £20." Henryson
also shows that the special sanctity attaching to absolution
granted by a Grey Friar was closely allied to the personality
of the Confessor :—

> " Ze ar mirrour, lanterne, and sicker way,
> Suld gide sic sempill folk as me to grace ;
> Zour bairfeit, and zour russat coule of gray,
> Zour lene cheik, zour paill pietious face,
> Schawis to me zour perfite halienes ;
> For weill war him that anis in his lyfe,
> Had hap to zow his sinnis for to schrive."

There are two letters to the Pope, one by James IV. and the other by his son and successor, James V., which, although they savour much of ecclesiastical rhetoric, testify to the value of the evangelical work of the Observant friars. In the first, dated 1st February 1506–7, James IV. asserts that "by their care the salvation of souls is here most diligently advanced, the negligence of others more fully remedied, the sacraments administered, and the word of Christ spread abroad by the lips of the faithful "; while James V., by petition dated 6th March 1531–32, informs His Holiness that the Order, " by the holiness and purity of its life, shines and is resplendent in the eyes of all men, and has ever been held in the highest veneration by our late illustrious father and by ourselves. We do not think it outwith our duty to be the Guardian, Defender, and Protector of that Order." It is, however, from the rugged verses of our reformer, Sir David Lindsay, that the distinction between the friars and the general body of the clergy is best appreciated. He condemns in vigorous verse all the Roman hierarchy and beneficed clergy for the absolute neglect of their holy offices, and for their refusal either to teach or preach. He tells us that—

> "They send furth freris to preche for thame,
> Quhilk garris the peple now abhor thame."

Nor is he less explicit in his testimony to the value of the evangelical work accomplished by the friars :—

> "War nocht the precheing of the begging freris,
> Tynt war the faith among the seculeris."

He marvels at the Bishop's want of shame—

> "To gyf yow freris sic preheminens
> Tyll vse thare office, to thare gret diffame,
> Precheing for thame in opin audiens."

He holds up to scorn the village parson who glories in a life of idleness and pleasure, and employs " ane Freir to preiche into my place " :—

> "Thocht I preiche not, I can play at the caiche ;
> I wot thair is nocht ane amang you all,
> Mair ferilie can play at the fut-ball :
> And for the carts, the tabils, and the dyse,
> Above all persouns I may beir the pryse."

And he thus completes the case of the whole of the clergy— " all the Spiritual state " :—

> "Pryde haith chaist far frome thame Humilitie.
> *Devotioun is fled unto the Freris,*
> Sensuale plesour hes baneist Chaistitie."

That the general body of the clergy, during the period of thirty years prior to the Reformation, continued in a condition of moral degradation is admitted by all writers, Roman and Protestant alike ; but Lindsay tells us—

> "Than Chastitie wald na langer abyde,
> *So, for refuge, fast to the freris scho fled,*
> Quhilks said they wald of ladys tak no cur,"

and she thereupon betook herself to the Black Sisters of the Convent of Siena on the Burgh Muir of Edinburgh. The friars, to whom Lindsay here refers, were the Edinburgh Observatines, who, under their Rules, could not undertake the " cure " or charge of women. Their friends, the Black Friars, reserved a special guest-house for lady visitors, built outside their priory walls.

The death of James v. in December 1542, and the appointment of the Earl of Arran to the Regency was quickly followed by the ascendancy of the Anglophile faction and the arrest of Cardinal Betoun. The year 1543, therefore, opened with a complete change in the political as well as the religious horizon. The reformed doctrines were openly professed, and the Bible was read in sympathy with the adoption by the Governor of the reformed doctrines. Attached to his suite were two apostate Black Friars of an aggressive type, Friars Williams and Rough, against whom the Edinburgh Observatines conducted a vigorous campaign in their sermons in the public streets. Knox tells us that they " yelled and rored as devillis in hell, Heresy ! Heresy ! Guyliame and Rought will cary the Governour to the Dewill," and he adds in explanation that " The toune of Edinburgh, for the most parte, was drouned in superstitioun." That the ancient Church, however, still maintained its hold over the citizens of Edinburgh became more apparent in the course of a few months. In the beginning of September, Arran suddenly left the city, when the infantry captains and others in his pay, at the instigation, it is believed, of Sadler, the English ambassador, made their way to the Black Friars with the intention of destroying it. The burghers, both men and women, however, rose up at the sound of the common bell, and " expulsed the said capitaynes out of the towne." Sadler in his official report declares that he " never saw people so wylde and in suche furye as they be here even now ! " By this time Arran had joined the Queen Dowager at Stirling, where, after undergoing penance at the hands of Betoun in the Grey Friary there, he was again received within the fold of the Catholic Church. Owing to the repudiation by the Scots of the proposed marriage between the infant Queen Mary and Prince Edward, the city was completely destroyed by fire in May 1544 by an English force under the command of the Earl of Hertford. The Grey Friary lay directly under the protection of the guns of the Castle, and there is some probability that on this occasion it escaped the fate meted out to the remainder of the city. In 1549 the meeting of the Provincial Council of the Church was held in the Black Friary at the east end of the Cowgate, and was attended by sixty members, including at least four representatives of the Observatines. Among the clergy present was the youthful Prior of St. Andrews, afterwards better known as the Earl of Moray. Various statutes for the reformation of the Church were passed; but the disease was too deep to be eradicated by mere words.

Concealed behind an all but impenetrable cloud of anonymity, little is known of the personality of the wardens or friars who studied in the schools or passed a period of their brotherhood at the Edinburgh friary. There were schools of philosophy and theology maintained for the instruction of the brethren; while the novices were sent to the friary at St. Andrews. As the parent house of the Observance, it was the custodier of the seal of the whole Province, and the customary residence of the Provincial Minister, as well as of the Visitor who corrected the Province on behalf of the Minister-General. Within its walls Robert Reid, Bishop of Orkney, and founder of the University of Edinburgh, received in 1526 the Cistercian habit and anointment as Abbot of Kinloss at the hands of Gavin Dunbar, the well-known Bishop of Aberdeen; and thirteen years later, when promoted to his See, there is reason to believe that Bishop Reid was also consecrated in the friary church. Of the friars themselves we know that Thomas Johnson died when battling the pestilence that ravaged the country in 1545; and the names of George Lythtone, Andrew Cairns, and Ludovic Williamson, who all abandoned the guidance of the Province in their extreme old age, alone survive to indicate the high regard in which the Edinburgh friary—the Mecca of the Observants—was held, as well as the custom of burying distinguished members before the high altar of the friary church. Friar Williamson, at the extreme age of eighty-eight, travelled from Stirling to the friary; and, if it be not apocryphal vaticination, we may believe with the chronicler that he summoned the Magistrates to his bedside, and, after warning them that the leading members of the realm would withdraw their allegiance from their spiritual as well as their temporal head, addressed an earnest appeal to them to remain steadfast in the old faith. But the evidences of the advance of the reformed religion were at this date only too apparent. A forcible illustration of the anti-clerical temper of the times was given on 1st September 1558, at the annual civic festival of St. Giles. The image of the saint had been stolen from St. Giles and thrown into the Nor' Loch, whence it had been rescued and committed to the flames. In this emergency a small statue of the Saint was borrowed from the church of the Observatines, and made secure with iron clamps to the " fertorie " on which it was to be carried. Attended by all the clergy and friars resident in the city, the statue was borne with tabrons and trumpets, banners and bagpipes through the principal streets. " And who was there to lead the ring," says Knox in his rugged, humorous account, " but the Queen Regent herself, with all her shavelings for honour of that feast." The Queen Regent, however, had no sooner left than the mob made a violent onslaught on " Little St. Giles," as they contemptuously styled the borrowed image, which was soon smashed, and the whole procession broken up. Then, as Knox describes with rollicking enjoyment, " doun goes the croses, of goes the surpleise, round caps corner with the crownes. The Gray Freiris gapped, the Black Frearis blew, the Preastis panted and fled, and happy was he that first gate the house."

Contemporary record clearly indicates that the Observatines represented the most healthy, the most disinterested, and, it may be affirmed, the most popular phase of ecclesiastical activity ; and it is easy to understand the reason why the Reformers selected the Observatines and the Black Friars for their first overt action against the Church. These two organisations formed the main bulwark on which the whole edifice at this time rested ; and, on their destruction, the superstructure naturally fell into ruins.

John Knox arrived at Leith on the 2nd of May 1559, and

D

nine days later the sack of the friaries at Perth was enacted. On the 14th, the Queen Dowager issued strict injunctions to the Town Council of Edinburgh to " gif gude heid and attendance that na sic uproir nor seditioun rys within your toun, bot that the religious places be surelie keptit." Lord Seton, as Provost, accordingly made provision for the defence of both the Grey and the Black Friaries, and, for greater security, he himself slept every night in one or other, and thereby became the cause of much offence to the Reformers. News reached the city on the 28th of June of the near approach of the Reformers, whereupon the destructive hand of the ever-willing " rascal multitude " soon reduced the two friaries to a mass of ruins. Knox furnishes the best account of the incident. He says :—

" The Provost for that tyme, the Lord Seytoun, a man without God, without honestie, and oftentymes without reasone, had befoir greatlie trubled and molested the bretherin ; for he had taikin upoun him the protectioun and defence of the Blak and Gray Frearis ; and for that purpose did nocht onelie lye him self in the one everie nicht, but also constraned the most honest of the town to wache those monstouris, to thair greaf and truble. But, hearing of our suddane cuming, he abandoned his charge, and left the spoile to the poore, who had maid havock of all suche thingis as was movable in those placis befoir our cuming, and had left nothing bot bair wallis, yea, nocht sa muche as door or windok ; wharthrow we war less trubilled in putting ordour to suche places."

It was one of these " most honest of the town " that was convicted of throwing stones, when on duty, at the priory windows.

On the destruction of their home, the friars obtained temporary shelter among those of their friends and adherents who were still to be found in the city ; and there they awaited with patience the result of the conflict outside the walls of

Edinburgh between the French and the English. Their presence in the burgh in the spring of 1560 is testified by the usual payment to them by the Comptroller of one chalder of barley and another of wheat ; but the death of the Queen Dowager, the departure of the French, and the passing of the statute of the 24th August by the Scottish Estates sealed their fate. The authority of the Pope in this country was abolished, and the celebration of the Mass forbidden under certain stringent enactments. In this, the supreme crisis in their history, the difference between the Conventual Grey Friars and their Observatine brethren became apparent. The Conventuals proved themselves more patriotic Scotsmen at heart than Churchmen ; while the Observatines were bound by fewer ties of affection or sentiment to the soil. They were idealists with their eyes fixedly centred on their Church, which they regarded in every sense of the word as their fatherland. Thus, when dispossessed of their friaries, they preferred exile to the repudiation of their faith ; and, accordingly, in the course of the summer of 1560, under the leadership of their last Provincial Minister, Father John Patrick, eighty Observatines—including in their number the Edinburgh Grey Friars—sailed from Scotland to the Netherlands, where they received a kindly welcome from the local Provincial, Father Francis Immomelanus. To them, as the birthplace of their Observance, that country had a special attraction. By the year 1563 they were settled in the various convents of the Province, one of their wardens, Robert Richard, having been received into the friary of Louvain on 1st September 1560 ; while Thomas Motto was appointed to teach in the friaries of the Province of Lower Germany. The tide of Observatine emigration may, therefore, have commenced shortly after the Treaty of Edinburgh. One or two of the Edinburgh friars certainly did remain in this country. During the winter of the year 1560–61, by the order of the Privy Council, all the members of the Mendicant Orders who chose to remain in Scotland under the new régime were each paid annually for their maintenance the sum of £16 Scots. Down to 1567 this pension was paid by the Lord Treasurer, and, subsequent to that date, out of the civic purse. From the respective records we learn that there were eight Grey and Black Friars belonging to Edinburgh who were in receipt of this pension. Four of these can be identified as Black Friars ; and, therefore, at least one or two of the Edinburgh Grey Friars must have remained in the country, and, in all probability, conformed to the tenets of the new religion.

"THE DEAD POVERELLO," BY ZURBARAN.

IV

THE GRAVEYARD—1560 TO 1612

On the dissolution of the ancient Church by the statute of 24th August 1560, and the departure of the friars to the Netherlands, their sole legacy to the town consisted of the ruined friary buildings and their yards. The Town Council were keenly on the alert, and in the Dean of Guild's Accounts for the half-year ending October 1560, payments are entered for the conveyance of some of the stones from the friary to be utilised in the erection of a new doorway at St. Giles. In April 1561, the Council resolved that, in view of the crowded condition of the burial-ground at St. Giles, " ane buriall place be maid farer fra the myddis of the toun, sic as in the Gray Freir Yaird, and the samyn biggit and maid close." A petition was accordingly presented to the young Queen Mary requesting a grant of the friary and its yards, "being sumquhat distant fra oure toun, to mak ane buriale place of to burie and eird the

HANGING LOCK OF THE BURIAL YET, 1613. DUG UP IN THE CHURCHYARD IN 1841.

personis deceissand thairin, sua that thairthrow the air within oure said toun may be the mair pure and clean." The royal sanction was obtained on 17th August 1562, and within a fortnight steps were taken to carry out the intentions of the Council. The corn sown by a squatter on the East Yard was seized, and Sir Edward Henderson was appointed master of works. A new boundary wall was built on the line of the old friary wall from the entrance at the Grassmarket, and brought round the corner until it joined that of the Uppermost Yard; while the street in front was levelled and causewayed. The old gateway was built up, and another, known as the

"Burial Yet," was erected on the site of the present entrance at the foot of the Candlemaker Row. We learn from the Burgh Records that "the greit yet quhare the new Tolbuith is beigit, [is] tane doune and hounge upon the entress at the Gray freir kirkyeard dike." For this imported gate there was provided in 1613 a hanging lock which in the course of centuries became lost, and was dug up in the graveyard so late as the year 1841 ; and over the entrance the following doggerel lines were placed in the course of the seventeenth century :—

> "Remember, Man, as thou goes by;
> As thou art now, so once was I;
> As I am now, so shalt thou be;
> Remember, Man, that thou must die."

The slope upward from the gate to the burial-ground was shortly afterwards replaced by stone steps, and, after the occupation of the church in 1620, the present roadway thence was made and causewayed. By the year 1565 the whole of the friary buildings were cleared away, and the stones utilised either for the new Tolbooth, or for building the dike round the graveyard at St. Giles. In 1566 a great hole in the outer wall of the friary yard through which the people, young and old, "clam in and furth," was filled up.

It has to be explained, however, that down to the year 1591, burials were only permitted in the northern half of the cemetery. The old Croft or Uppermost Yard of the friars was retained in the hands of the Magistrates, who, on 13th September 1566, leased it for four years to Bailie John Sym. The obligations imposed under the lease on the worthy bailie are somewhat peculiar, and raise him in modern eyes to the position of a public benefactor. He was to rebuild the mid-dike between the "buriall place and the said yeard "; and to insert a door in the eastern wall. Through this door, if provided at his own expense with a key, every "honest man"—i.e. good citizen—could enter to "periurnie, gang, rest,

THE MARTYRS' MONUMENT.

and pas thair tyme in the yeard foirsaid *gratis* " ! The town reserved the right to hold " wapinschaws " or other conventions, and to " mak thair buriall thairunto geve necessitie requyre." The first wapinschaw or parade of troops in the Uppermost Yard took place on 7th July 1571. It was at the time when the gallant and chivalrous Kirkaldy of Grange held the Castle on behalf of the unfortunate and hapless Queen Mary. The provost, bailies, and many of the burghers had joined the Regent Lennox at Leith : but the unknown chronicler tells us that, to the number of about six hundred, " the haill merchandis, craftismen, and personis remanand within Edinburgh maid thair moustaris in the gray frear kirk yaird ; promitting to assist the capitane of Edinburgh castell in the quenis actioun." [1] Two years later the then Regent, James, Earl of Morton, made application to Queen Elizabeth for assistance, and a small army, accompanied by a powerful train of artillery under the command of Sir William Drury, was sent into Scotland. This force reached Edinburgh on 25th April 1573, and, after an unsuccessful attempt to seduce Kirkaldy from his allegiance, the siege of the Castle proceeded. Under the cover of night, five batteries in different positions round the fortress were erected, and we learn that " on the croftis of the gray freris, callit Lawson's croft, lay thrie gross culvering," [2] or large guns. This battery was intended to take King David's Tower in flank, and must have stood about fifty feet north of the present recorder's office, and at right angles to the footpath that leads to the Martyrs' Monument. The powerful artillery of the English soon reduced the defences of the Castle to ruins, and on 28th May Kirkaldy was forced to surrender. He was subsequently executed by Morton, and with his death the cause of the Scottish Queen became hopeless. The identity of Lawson, the tenant of the Uppermost Yard, is unknown, although

[1] *Diurnal of Occurrents*, p. 231.   [2] *Ibid.* p. 331.

SIEGE OF EDINBURGH CASTLE, 1573. BATTERY OF THREE GROSS CULVERINGS, UPPER GREYFRIARS' YARD.
From Contemporary Drawing. *Bann. Club Misc.*, vol. ii.

it may be asserted that he had no connection with the Lawsons of Highriggs, whose name is still commemorated in Lady Lawson Street. Curiously enough, Morton himself was the first person of note who found a last resting-place within the precincts of the Greyfriars' Cemetery. He was executed on 2nd June 1581 by the instrument known as the Maiden, now preserved in the National Museum of Antiquities; and, while his head was stuck upon an iron spike at the Old Tolbooth, his body was carried off during the night-time and buried in the Greyfriars. The Douglases were a powerful and active family, and in December of the following year his head was removed by command of the Privy Council and placed in the same grave with the body. The next celebrity to be interred was George Buchanan, the famous Latin scholar. He died on 28th September 1582, and his funeral was attended by " a large company of the faithful." The *through stone* which marked his place of sepulture in the course of time sank underneath the surface of the ground, and was raised by order of the Town Council in 1701; but it has now entirely disappeared, and the tablet, which was set up about sixty years ago, may be held to mark the probable site of the grave.[1] He was buried in the East Yard of the friars, which extended northward to within a few yards of the present Martyrs' Monument. The ground to the west of the latter was utilised as the common burial-ground, and, ultimately, that for malefactors, among whom, in the seventeenth century, were included the Covenanting martyrs executed during the Episcopalian ascendancy. There seems at first to have been no supervision exercised over the people in their use of the graveyard. The graves were dug, and the burials made by the parties interested; and it was not until January 1583–84 that the Town Council appointed a proper grave-

[1] See the scholarly account of the Graveyard by the late Dr. Laing, in preface to Brown's *Epitaphs and Mon. Inscrip. in Greyfriars' Churchyard.*

E

digger—" ane man to mak and cast the graivis, gadder and
burie the baynes, and keep the kirk-zaird." The mis-
behaviour of the people " quhome the bailyies can nocht
oversie without greitt danger "—owing to the plague—became
so great that the Magistrates closed the Greyfriars as a place
of sepulture, and ordered all burials to be made in the
" Nether yaird of the Hie Kirk "—St. Giles—" for a season."
Two months later, on 10th September 1585, this order was
rescinded, the Nether Kirk Yard at St. Giles closed up—
probably for the last time—and burial permitted as before
in the Greyfriars' Yard. On the 20th July 1587 a second
wapinschaw was held in the Uppermost Yard by the provost
and bailies, " of all maner of persouns, indwellaris within
this burgh, boddin in feare of weir, and arayet in thair best
airmour"; and, by an Act passed on 15th March 1590–91,
the Council agreed to permit the bodies of Alexander Clerk,
an ex-provost, and David Kynloch, a baxter or baker, to
" be bureit in the Ovir Kirk Yaird in the Greyfreiris, begyn-
nand at sic part as the Dene of Gild sall think maist expedient." These were the first interments in the Upper or Over
Yard, and the Council at the same time ordained "that nane
other be bureit thair heirafter without the avyse of the
Counsall." The demand for increased space for burial soon
became so urgent that in a year or two the Town Council
were obliged to throw open the Upper or Over Yard for the
use of the public. It is to be noticed that our economical
Town Council were in the practice of leasing the grass of the
graveyard; but in the winter of 1586–87 the rent or duty
was remitted on account of the prevalence of the plague.
In 1596 the grass was leased to one Home for a sum of £45.
The last relics of the ancient friars consisted now of their two
wells, which, in 1591, were ordered to be cleaned out for the
use of the inhabitants. In 1596–97, for greater convenience,
a spout was inserted in the outer wall of the graveyard, and
a "punchoun to kep the watter in" was placed underneath.

GEORGE BUCHANAN'S MONUMENT.

Erected by Dr DAVID LAING.

V

CONGREGATION OF THE SOUTH-WEST PARISH

Although the Greyfriars' Church may be taken to have been founded in the year 1612, the Congregation itself was formed at an earlier period. Twenty years after the successful issue of the Reformation, the amount of church accommodation in Edinburgh proved inadequate for the requirements of the citizens; and, in 1584, the Town Council passed an Act under which the city was to be divided into four parishes, with " a competent kirk to everie parochein." No action followed on this resolution, and six years later, on the petition of the City Kirk Session, the Council agreed to increase the number of parishes to eight. The City Fathers, however, were not to be forced into any definite action involving expense, until in 1597 they ordered intimation of the division into eight parishes to be made to the General Assembly, and ministers to be appointed. The King, James VI., was desirous of destroying the power and influence of the coterie of ministers who filled the pulpits in St. Giles, and he was present in the " grate Kirk of Edinburgh " on Sunday, 17th February 1597–98, when Mr. Patrick Galloway read out the form or manner of the " four kirkis of Edinburgh, ane quarter of the toune to everie kirke." [1] The division into four quarters or parishes accordingly took place, and, on 18th May 1598, the High or Upper Tolbooth Church at the west end of St. Giles was allocated to the congregation of the parish of what was then called the South-West Quarter —afterwards the Greyfriars' Parish—and Messrs. Robert Rollock and Peter Hewat appointed as its ministers.[2] It is, therefore, to be understood that, before the erection of the Greyfriars' Church, the congregation worshipped in

[1] Birrell's *Diary*, p. 42.   [2] Calderwood's *History*, p. 713.

the Upper Tolbooth, and that the parish is still designated as the " South-West or Greyfriars' Parish." The name " South-West Quarter" appears in connection with St. Giles as early as the year 1563 ; but no special ministers or parish were attached to it. One authority asserts errone- ously that, for a short period, the South-West congregation occupied the Magdalene Chapel in the Cowgate.[1] On the 26th, orders were issued that the " parpall wall in the eist end of the *hie kirke* betuixt ye same and ye vtter Tolbuith be tayne doun and set eister mair to ye next gang of pillers, yat ye said Tolbuith may serve for ane Interim [Church] mair commodiouslie to the south west quarter "; and, seven months later, for the construction of seats and lofts in the church as well as for a pulpit. Some difficulties, however, in the taking down of this " parpall " or partition wall occurred with the workmen, who refused to undertake the work either at a fixed price for the whole, or by measurement —" upon task or by the ruid beam." The new extended wall was built, but, in July of the following year, the Council found it necessary to apply for royal authority in order to force the workmen to remove the " auld parpall wall." The precise *locale* of the High Tolbooth Church in which the congregation of the South-West Parish worshipped has hitherto been a matter of some doubt; but the above excerpts from the City Records identify it as one of the sections, the western, into which St. Giles was divided. To carry out the necessary alterations at St. Giles, the Council borrowed from the Trinity Hospital Fund the sum of 1200 merks.

Robert Rollock, the first minister of the first charge of the South-West Parish, was the son of David Rollock, laird of Powis, near Stirling, and in 1583 was appointed by the Town Council to be the first rector or principal of their newly founded College or University of Edinburgh,

[1] Hew Scott, *Fasti Eccl. Scot.*, i. p. 39.

to which King James gave his name—his sole gift. Rollock died in February 1599 at the early age of forty-three, and has been described as a man of great erudition, singular piety, and integrity of life. He was succeeded by Mr. Peter Hewat, the minister of the second charge, whose stipend paid by the Council amounted at this time to the small sum of 500 merks. It was increased in 1605 to 800 merks, in addition to a free house; and in 1616 there was a general augmentation of the stipends of the ministry to 1200 merks Scots, or £66, 13s. 4d. sterling—a sum which, though small, was of much greater value in those days than the amount betokens. At the request of the King, Hewat was translated to the East or Little Kirk some time after February 1610. He afterwards took part in the revisal of the proposed new liturgy, and in 1617 he drew up a Protest for the Liberties of the Kirk, for his adherence to which he was deprived of his office. His successor was Mr. Andrew Ramsay of the family of Balmain.[1] In his younger days, Ramsay had prosecuted his theological studies in France, and had occupied a professorial chair in the University of Saumur. In 1613 the Town Council obtained authority from the Archbishop of St. Andrews, directing him to proceed to Edinburgh to stand his " trial " as one of the city ministers; and he was duly appointed on the 28th April of the following year to the pulpit of the South-West Congregation at a stipend of 1000 merks *per annum*, with an allowance for house rent. Three years afterwards, the house occupied by the widow of Walter Balcanquhal—a well-known minister at St. Giles— was handed over to him, and the allowance for " house mail " thereupon ceased. He continued his ministrations in the High Tolbooth Church until the month of December

[1] There is considerable difficulty regarding the appointment of Mr. Ramsay, as, prior to 1620, the City Record fails to identify the parish of his ministry; but it is believed that he must have been the successor of Hewat.

1620, when the new church at the Greyfriars was formally taken over by the South-West Congregation. It is remarkable that, although Mr. Ramsay took a prominent part in the furtherance of the Covenant, all our authorities —including the *Fasti*—contain divergent accounts of the details of his ministry.

VI

ERECTION OF THE GREYFRIARS' CHURCH

The arrangement of 1598 failed to meet the requirements of the citizens in the matter of church accommodation; and, accordingly, in November 1601, the City Kirk-Sessions persuaded the Town Council to agree, by plurality of votes, that " ye rowme and plaice in ye buriall yaird qr sometyme was situat ye gray freiris " was " ye maist meitt and convenient plaice for bigging of ane new kirk yairon." In the beginning of the following year, the Council again recognised the suitability of the Graveyard as a site for the new church, and resolved " yat ye samyn should be biggit in ye heiche yard." The sum of £500 was set aside for this purpose, and the dimensions of the proposed church fixed at " ye lenth of six scoir fute and of ye breid of thre scoir futes." In July the buttresses and doors of the Nunnery at the Sciennes were ordered to be taken down and employed in " ye wark of ye new kirk in ye burial yaird "[1]; while, in October of the following year, " Patrick Cochrane, Maister of Wark in Grayfreris," was to pay to the Council " ye price of ye aisler staynes qlk wes in ye hie kirk yaird, and ye said Baillies to give it to the poor." Then, in the City Treasurer's accounts for 1603–4, a payment is noted to Richard Forrest and two work-

[1] *Council Records*, xi. 94.

OLD GREYFRIARS' CHURCH—South-East View.

men "for careing the haill grit stainis in the buriall
place to the new kirk wall of ye gray freiris." We probably find here the kernel of the mythical story related
by Chambers that the gravestones in St. Giles' Churchyard
were removed thence, and re-erected in the Greyfriars.
A sum of 200 merks received in alms from Hugh Brown,
one of the partners of the Cunzie House—the Mint—was
also handed over to Cochrane as the receiver of monies for
the building of the church. Eight years afterwards the
Council ordained that the "kirk foundit in the buriall
yaird be biggit with pilleris." It is evident that, down to
the year 1611, not a stone of the building had been laid, and
that our poor but shrewd City Fathers were, by the passing
of these resolutions, skilfully marking time. A change in
the religious aspect of the situation had occurred by this
time through the establishment in the country of Episcopacy,
and the order of the King that the pulpits of all the churches
in Edinburgh should be patent to " all Bishops at all tymes
whensoever they pleased to teach." [1] Aided by a bequest
from John Layng of 500 merks, the Council finally consented,
on 23rd December 1612, to give practical effect to their
resolutions. Failing to obtain the necessary timber for
the building either in the west country or in Ireland, the
Council in 1611 commissioned Thomas Watson, a merchant
burgess of Edinburgh, to purchase the timber in Sweden.
Watson was successful in his errand, and loaded two ships
with a cargo of wood. Unfortunately for him, a state of
war existed at the time between the Swedes and Danes,
and on the voyage homewards the ships " wer persewit,
tane, and maid lauchfull pryse " by the Danish men-of-
war. An unsuccessful appeal was thereupon made for
restitution on behalf of Watson by the Scottish Privy
Council to King James,[2] and, accordingly, in 1614, there
appears a notice in the City Records of an agreement with

[1] Row's *Hist.*, p. 110.   [2] *Privy Council Reg.*, ix. p. 620.

a Dutchman[1] for the supply of timber for the roof of the church. On a panel on the east gable the date 1614 is marked; while, according to Wilson, the north-eastern pillar bore the year 1613. In 1616 a sum of 2000 merks from the Trinity Hospital was, along with other sums, borrowed to be employed in the building of the church; but by this time the work was approaching completion. The economical Council placed in the church the pulpit belonging to the High School, and in 1618 a copy of the Bible was purchased, and, along with the keys of the church, a green cloth and the book of accounts, handed over to the care of the Dean of Guild. At the same time, a request was tendered to the City Kirk-Sessions to relieve the Council of all the monies borrowed from the Hospital Fund for the use of the church. In the following year the church was temporarily opened for the purpose of celebrating the obsequies of the well-known William Couper, Bishop of Galloway. Calderwood narrates that "upon the 18th of February [1619], his corps was carried to the Grayfriers with sound of trumpets. The Bishop of St. Androes made the funerall sermoun in the Grayfrier Kirk. It was noe wonder to heare one Bishope speak to the praise of another."[2] Four months later a bequest by one William Justice of 100 merks towards the completion of the church was taken possession of by the City Treasurer. At last, on 1st December 1620, the Town Council passed an Act that—" owing to the increas of the inhabitants of the burgh, and the concourse of noblemen, gentlemen, etc., repairing to the same at the Sessions and other public conventions, the three churches presently occupied are not of sufficient capacity to hold those who resort to public sermons, nor the present pastor able to overtake the charge—therefore, the new Kirk in the Gray freiris be opened also, and that public preaching on Sabbath day in before and afternoon take

[1] *Council Records*, xii. 150.   [2] Calderwood, vii. 349–51, Wod. Soc.

place there, Andrew Ramsay and the other ministers of the burgh to supply the preaching until a competent number of pastors be planted. And that the Counsell cause the principal of thair College—as he is obliged—to supply the place on the Sabbath afternoon in the new Grayfrier Kirk, and that the week days be supplied by thair ordinary pastors." Calderwood tells us that the City Kirk-Sessions appointed Patrick Galloway, the minister of the High Church, to open the church with public worship on Sunday, the 17th; but, alleging that both it and the Sunday following were "dismal" days, he fixed upon Christmas as the proper day for the opening service. He gave as his reason for the alteration "the preaching of the angels to the Sheepheards, and praising of God that day," and, he pointedly added, "it behoved him to say some thing for holie days, *to please the King*."[1] When minister at Perth, he was so Puritanic that, according to Calderwood, he "would not eat a *Christmas* pie." Galloway in religion was a small Vicar of Bray, and, at this period, stood in high favour with the King. Even after the opening of the church some further alterations were found necessary. A portal or porch was built at the east door, the interior was painted, a baptismal basin or font and cloth provided, and the pillar of repentance built at a cost of £48, 13s. 4d. Scots. In the City Accounts for 1626, a payment of eight shillings is entered "to David Weir for caryeing of communioune buirdis fra ye Ald Kirk to ye Grayfrier Kirk," and another of ten shillings "for ane ald manns heid"— whatever that may mean—"to James Marjoribanks for ye Grayfreir Kirk." The communion table here referred to stood on a stone platform which was replaced by woodwork so late as the year 1794. Two donations towards the erection of the Church fall here to be noticed. The first was a legacy[2] of £20 granted in 1621 by Thomas Dickson, a

---

[1] Calderwood, vii. 454.   [2] *Council Records*, xiii. 137.

F

maltman in Edinburgh; while the second consisted of a sum of £110 " quhilk was ane pairt of the sowmes collectit be the ministris of this burgh for the use of the kirk in the Gray frieris." [1]

The church itself—the net product of nineteen years' care and labour by our City Fathers—cannot be said to evince on their part any instinctive genius for architecture or desire for extravagant display in stone and lime. Patrick Cochrane, the Master of Works, was probably a builder; but the style, or want of style, in its construction clearly points to the decadent condition of Gothic architecture in the beginning of the seventeenth century. Indeed, it is only to the erection of the two masterpieces, Sir Walter Scott's monument and the spire of the Assembly Hall—the former designed by Kemp, and the latter by Pugin—that the recent revival in this branch of architecture is due. The employment of the stones taken from the Nunnery at the Sciennes and from the kirkyard of St. Giles in the building of its rough rubble walls, and the other makeshifts, such as the transference of the pulpit from the High School and the communion table from the Old Church, sufficiently denote the thrifty atmosphere that pervaded the Council Board of those days. From the drawing of Gordon of Rothiemay of 1647, an idea can be obtained of the form of the church as originally designed. There were three entrances. On the north was a large doorway—still in use—to which a causewayed road from the " burial yet " at the foot of Candlemaker Row was made in 1621. In the middle of the eastern wall was another door, the outlines of which still remain; and on the south was a third which was converted in 1696 into a window. In the western gable a window was inserted; while in the ungainly tower a clock— or " knock," to use the words of the old record—was placed. The principal entrance gateway from Greyfriars' Place

1 *Council Records*, xiii. 175.

to the churchyard—" the greit entrie to the Grayfrier Kirk over against the Societie "—was constructed in 1624, and, on the erection of the recorder's office, a handsome monument erected in 1616 to the memory of Alexander Miller, Master Tailor to James VI., was removed.

VII

GREYFRIARS' CHURCH—1620 TO 1638

It was, therefore, in December 1620 that the congregation of the South-West Parish of Edinburgh bade adieu to their old quarters in the High Tolbooth Church at St. Giles, and transferred themselves under their minister, Mr. Andrew Ramsay—a name to become famous in the annals of the Church—to the new building in the Greyfriars' Churchyard. Thenceforth, both church and parish became known under the name of the Greyfriars. Under the arrangement with the Council, Mr. Ramsay preached in the forenoon, the afternoon service being undertaken by the Principal of the University. The Principal at this date was Patrick Sandis, who undertook the " supply " in the Sunday afternoons down to August 1622, when he resigned his office. His successor was Mr. Robert Boyd, who was stoutly opposed to the Episcopalian schemes of King James, and under the royal commands was forced to resign the Principalship, with its attendant office of minister of the second charge at Greyfriars. On 22nd July 1621, Alexander Simson, minister at Mertoun, preached in Greyfriars, and delivered a violent diatribe against the King. It appears that our Scottish Solomon, who professed to tremble at the sight of a naked sword, was not averse to the use of strong language. Calderwood tells us that Simson " spared neither King, Bishop, nor Minister, and found fault with the watchmen of both countries [England as well as Scotland] for not admonishing the King to forbeare his oaths [give up his habit of swearing]"; and that, when called before the Privy Council, he dubbed the bishops that were present "belligods, and enemies to the Kirk of Christ." He was so vituperant that, when removed, he was "not called in againe" but sent a prisoner to Dumbarton Castle, "their to remayne prosonner till he be examat as said is." [1] During the following year there was a great dearth of provisions in Edinburgh, and the Town Council, as a token of affection, granted to five of the City ministers—including in that number Mr. Andrew Ramsay—a special gift of 200 merks. In 1625, the city was again formally divided into four parishes, with two ministers to each; [2] and it was also ordained that the Principal of the University was not to be included among the latter. Accordingly, the South-West Parish under Mr. Ramsay was once more relegated to the Greyfriars, and an additional minister was ordered to be provided with all expedition. The Council also appointed that the weekly preachings should be held "upon tysday in the South West Kirk," and that the session of the "South West parochin be haldin ilk Tyisday in the efternoone at Tua houris, efternoone, in the south west or gray frier kirk." It is to be remembered that in the seventeenth century the Town Council claimed the right of supervision over the ongoings of the individual members of the kirk-sessions, as it did over those of the ministers. For example, fifty years later, the Council enacted that the "Elders and Deacons of ye Gray friers and oyrs [be] ordained punctually to attend their session dyets under pain of 40 lib. to the elder, and 20 to ye deacon"! Following upon the re-arrangement of the parishes, a drastic order was issued commanding all the citizens to resort to the kirk in their

---

[1] *Reg. of Privy Council*, xii. p. 545 and n.
[2] *Council Records*, xiii. 311.

respective parishes. It will be noticed from the "Inventar of the thingis belanging to ye kirkis of yis bur^t" handed over to the care of John Maknacht, the new Dean of Guild, that in 1626 the church had been supplied with a sand glass and a baptismal font :—

"Ye Greyfreir Kirk.

" *Item*, ane byble w^t ane sand glass,
    Item, ane greine claith for ye pulpitt,
    Item, ane litle greine buird claith w^t ane buird appoyn-
        tit for ye elderis and deykinis,
    Item, ane basoune w^t ane watter claith."

Entries appear in the City Accounts for 1626 and subsequent dates[1] for furnishing Greyfriars and the other three churches with flowers during the summer season, in order, presumably, to decorate the communion table—a beautiful practice, which has been recently revived. In 1631 the sum of £7 Scots is entered as paid to "ye lass yat furnishit flouris to ye kirkis." In the following year, as well as in 1630, the University graduation ceremonial—" ye tyme yat ye ministers wer maid "—was held in the church, with the usual result of destruction to the pews or stalls at the hands of the youthful and boisterous students.

In May 1629 the Council paid for some repairs to the church and its steeple, as well as to Mr. Ramsay's house or manse, and, in the following June, appointed Mr. Henry Rollock, a nephew of the first minister of the South-West congregation, to be coadjutor with Mr. Ramsay. He did not accept office, and in the following year James Fairlie, son of an " honest burgess of Edinburgh," was elected to the second charge in the Greyfriars. Fairlie is described as a man of " good, able spirit," and in 1607, when only a youth of nineteen, he was appointed a Regent in Philosophy in the University, and, in 1629, Professor of Divinity.

[1] Dean of Guild's Accounts.

During the years 1631 to 1634 gratuities were paid by
the Council to each of the ministers of the burgh, thereby
evincing the complete inadequacy of their stipends.   In
1633 Edinburgh was erected by Charles i. into a bishopric,
with St. Giles as the Cathedral, and the names of the two
ministers of the Greyfriars were duly noted in the list of
the prebends.   During this decade, the name of Archibald
Johnston of Wariston appears frequently as a worshipper
in Greyfriars, and, in his recently discovered diary, the
personal characteristics of this remarkable man are vividly
portrayed.   Under the date 12th June 1634, for example,
he tells us that " In the Grayfriar Kirk I got tears ; and
thair we sang 143 and 144 Ps.   We read, not without
a providence, the 20 c. of 2 Chron., about Jehosophat,
' Lord, we know not what to doe.'   Mr. James Fairley in
his sermon spak mutch against sclandering and calum-
niating.   Betwixt sermons I got tears.   Afternoon we
sang 145 and 146 most fit Ps., and we heard Mr. Andrew
[Ramsay] on 11 c. of Math. 28 v. ' Come al ye,' etc.   After
sermon I got sundry tears." [1]   Carlyle describes him as
the " Redactor of the Covenanters' protests in 1637 and
onwards ; redactor, perhaps, of the Covenant itself ; canny,
lynx-eyed Lawyer, and austere Presbyterian Zealot ; full
of fire, of heavy energy and gloom ; in fact, a very notable
character."   There were no pews in Greyfriars at this
date, except a few stalls erected for the civic and other
dignitaries, and the elders.   Wariston and the other
worshippers sat on stools, and, during the delivery of the
sermon, the whole of the masculine portion of the congregation kept on their hats.   This was the common
practice both in England and Scotland ; and Mr. George
Gillespie, who afterwards occupied the pulpit of Greyfriars, in his description in 1637, says that " a man comming
into one of our churches in time of public worship, if he

[1] Wariston's *Diary*, S.H.Soc., 194.

Rev. GEORGE GILLESPIE,

Minister of Greyfriars (1641-1647),

From a Portrait in New College Hall, Edinburgh.

Photo by E. Drummond Young.

see the hearers covered, he knows by this customeable
signe that sermon is begunne." [1]   Indeed, it was not until
the beginning of the eighteenth century that the system
of keeping the head uncovered during the whole of the
service took its rise.   In many of our Scottish churches
even the minister, in imitation of the old custom on the
Continent, resumed his head-covering the moment he commenced his sermon, which his hearers, at least in some
instances, did not hesitate to punctuate with applause !
In the City Accounts for March 1634, payments are entered
for furnishing a lock and key to the " Lady Advocate's
seat," and for the making of three other seats ; while,
three years later, a payment is noted for erecting a great
bar at the back of the Town Council's seat, and for adorning
it with thirty-three little wooden pillars.   But it was not
until the end of December 1639 that the Council ordered
pews to be fitted up in all the City churches, and, at the
same time, imposed the charge now known as the " seat
rents." [2]   An entry in the Dean of Guild's Accounts for
8th February 1662 marks the first time the pews were
numbered for the purposes of identification—" Item, for
marking the seattis in the Grayfrier Kirk with coulers and
figures, xvi lib."   By an Act of the Town Council, dated
1st May 1635, a tax [3]—made notorious in the middle of the
nineteenth century in the annals of Edinburgh under the
name of the Annuity Tax—had been levied on the citizens
for the support of the ministers ; and, as the proceeds of the
tax had proved insufficient for this purpose, the seat rents
were ordered to be utilised as a further contribution in aid

[1] *Dispute against the English-Popish Ceremonies*, 1637, part iii. p. 86.

[2] Act of Council ordaining that the whole churches of this burgh shall be
fitted with pews or desks, and that a certain yearly duty be imposed on them
for help to pay the ministers' stipends, the usual funds not being sufficient.
Council Records, xv. 112, 29th December 1639.

[3] Levy on the whole inhabitants of this burgh (except Lords of Council and
Session) for the ministers' stipends.   *Council Records*, xiv. 386.

of the fund. During this year—1635—it is also interesting
to note that there were issued to " James Marjoribanks
for ye Gray freiris 1600 tickettis," or *tokens*, for the communion at Easter, and 1400 for that in August,[1] and it
may be stated in explanation that, out of a total of 5071
houses in Edinburgh at this date, the South-West parish
contained 1429, being a greater number than in any of
the other quarters or parishes.[2] The crowded condition
of the graveyard now began to excite the attention of the
Council, and by an Act of 1st April 1636, the large grass
park lying immediately to the south of the graveyard
was ordered to be " inclosed with ane toun wall," and
that to " be ane augmentatioune to the burrall zaird." [3]
In 1618 the town had purchased from Tours of Inverleith
ten acres Scots lying to the south of the Flodden Wall,
eight and a half acres of which were afterwards sold to
the Governors of George Heriot's Hospital. The grass
park formed the remaining portion left in the hands of
the Council; although it was only in 1636, as above
mentioned, that the City Wall, known as the Third or
Telfer's Wall, was finished round by Teviot Row to Bristo
Port. The piece of ground thus enclosed, extending from
Bristo Street on the east to the wall of Heriot's Hospital
on the west, measured between two and three acres *Imperial*, and became known under the general name of the
" Greyfriars' Yard," or, to differentiate it from the old
graveyard, as the " South," " Inner," " New," or " Back
Greyfriars' Yard." In point of fact, it was never utilised
as a graveyard until the beginning of the eighteenth century,
when a small strip of ground on the western side was given
off to form the "southern extension." Its historical
importance consists in the fact that it was in this large
park that, as will be afterwards noted, the Covenanting

[1] Dean of Guild's Accounts.   [2] Maitland, p. 70.
[3] *Council Records*, xiv. 375.

prisoners taken in 1679 at Bothwell Bridge were interned. During the interval it was leased by the town to tenants as a grass park, or used as a drilling-ground for the burghers, as well as for other purposes.

From the Dean of Guild's accounts for 1636–37 we learn that the pillar of repentance was provided with a door and a pair of " bands." Ten years earlier, the Dean had paid for " xii bowttis "—iron bars—" to ye pyller of repentance in ye Grayfrier Kirk," and for two pairs of bands; but there seems to be no mention in these accounts of the stool of repentance or the " pair " of sheets, without which our churches at this date would have been incomplete. The occupants of the repentance *stool*, unlike the other members of the congregation, sat " bare-heidit all the tyme of the sermons." [1] The last stool of repentance belonging to the Greyfriars—one of the

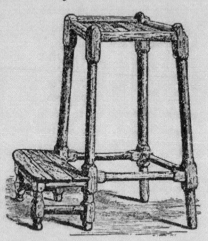

few remaining relics of its kind in the country—is now preserved in the National Museum of Antiquities. It was fortunately removed by the Reverend John Hepburn, minister of the second charge at Old Greyfriars between the years 1732 and 1749, at a time when these articles of Church discipline had fallen into desuetude. The great power which the ministers and kirk-sessions exercised, during the seventeenth and part of the eighteenth centuries, over the moral and

STOOL OF REPENTANCE FORMERLY USED IN THE GREYFRIARS' CHURCH, AND NOW PRESERVED IN THE NATIONAL MUSEUM OF ANTIQUITIES.

religious welfare of their parishioners, forms a striking

[1] *Book of the Universal Kirk*, i. 160.

G

feature in the domestic history of those days. In the year 1690, " all Acts enjoyneing civil paines upon sentences of excommunication " were repealed by the Scottish Parliament; but these ecclesiastical courts, however, continued to pronounce sentences which the Magistrates were only too ready to enforce by imprisonment. Thus, in the roll or minute book of the Edinburgh General Kirk-Sessions—which included that of the Greyfriars—there is an entry, dated 28th March 1699, to the effect that it had again been represented to the Magistrates and Sessions that " ye Lord's Day is profaned by peoples standing on the streets, and vaging to the fields, and standing idle gazing out of windows, and that children and prentices are seen playing in severall places." The Sessions thereupon ordained that " the parents or masters of such children or servants will be carried before the Kirk-Session and censured . . . and, if they do not amend, they will be referred to the Magistrates for punishment." [1] It was not until the year 1711 that this power was abolished by an Act of the British Parliament. This Act expressly forbade the granting by Church Courts in Scotland of civil pains and penalties incurred " by reason of any excommunication, or prosecution in order to excommunication " ; and it prohibited all civil magistrates from compelling any person " to appear when summoned, or to give obedience to any such sentence when pronounced." The passing of this Act was long deplored on the north side of the Tweed as " among the causes of the Lord's wrath against sinful and backsliding Scotland " ; and, in many instances, the Church Courts, despite the statute, continued for years thereafter to exercise their ancient rights! Even as late as the year 1792, fines or penalties were exacted from backsliders in a parish near Aberdeen.

The determined and long-continued efforts of King

[1] *General Kirk-Sessions Record.*

James, his son Charles, and the prelatic party to thrust upon an unwilling people the English forms of Church government and worship were at last approaching the final stage that presaged revolution. By an Act of the Scottish Parliament of 1606, James had been acknowledged supreme over all persons and causes; but he himself asserted his own authority to govern by the divine right of kings. "It is," he claimed, "a power innated, and a special prerogative which we that are Christian Kings have, to order and dispose of external things in the policy of the Church." The establishment in 1610 of what is known as the first Episcopal régime made little change in the practice and mode of public worship, as laid down in Knox's liturgy of 1564 and subsequent years; but the preparation of a new liturgy by the bishops, and, in particular, the passing, under royal pressure, of the famous five Articles of Perth, created fierce excitement, and James, who knew well the character of his countrymen, deemed it prudent to stay his hand. His son and successor, Charles I., under the inspiration of Laud, Archbishop of Canterbury, favoured the introduction of the English liturgical forms with the object of securing uniformity of worship on both sides of the Tweed; although, ultimately, he gave instructions to the Scottish bishops to prepare a new "Liturgy as near that of England as might be." The book, known to history as *Laud's Liturgy*, was duly compiled by Scottish Episcopal hands, and sent to Laud and the King for revision. That Laud exercised considerable influence in its compilation there can be no question, and the copy, containing many emendations in the handwriting of King Charles, is now in the possession of Lord Rosebery; but it was distinctly Scottish in its origin. Now, it is to be remembered that John Knox's liturgy made provision for the reading of certain prayers—including the Lord's Prayer—as well as for the use of extempore prayers, the doxology (*Gloria Patri* in English), the absolution, and the Apostles' Creed. The new liturgy was appointed to be read in St. Giles for the first time in the forenoon of the 23rd July 1637. At the reader's service, held at eight o'clock in the morning, the well-known Patrick Henderson read the prayers as printed in Knox's liturgy, according to the usual practice of the Church; and it was the reading of *Laud's Liturgy* at a later hour that led to the popular outburst with which, according to tradition, the name of Jenny Geddes is closely associated. The country, notwithstanding the appointment of bishops, was undoubtedly Presbyterian at heart; and the violent demonstration of popular indignation at St. Giles was mainly due to the repeated attempts to introduce " novations in religion "—pin-pricks—which were regarded as stepping-stones to Popery.

It was the intention of the bishops that the service-book should also have been read at the Greyfriars on the day of the fateful riot at St. Giles. Mr. Andrew Ramsay, the minister of the first charge, however, stoutly opposed the reading of the book, and, in consequence, he was called before the bishops and put to " silence." His co-adjutor, Fairlie, demitted his office on the 28th of July,[1] and was promoted to the bishopric of Argyll. This explains the statement made by Baillie that " On Sunday morning, when the Bishop and his Dean in the Great Church [and the] Bishop of Argyle in the Grayfriers, began to officiat, as they speak, incontinent the serving maids began such a tumult as was never heard of since the Reformation in our nation." It is evident that *Laud's Liturgy* was read on that eventful morning by Dean Hanna in St. Giles, as well as by Mr. Fairlie in the Church of the Greyfriars, and with disastrous results in both cases.[2] Baillie also mentions that, when the Commission was read, Ramsay

---

[1] *Council Records*, xv. 18.   [2] Baillie's *Letters*, i. 18.

alone had the courage to "flight" it. On the following Sunday, Ramsay refused to conduct the service at Greyfriars, and Wariston tells us that "upon the 30 of July, Sunday, thair was no service read at al, neyther old nor new, but ane humble sermon without prayers, chapters, psalmes. Mr. Hery Rollok and Mr. Andrew Ramsey refused the service."[1] William Row, the youngest son of the Church historian, alleges that his father, John Row, was the first to preach, after the beginning of the work of reformation, "in the Grayfrier Kirk, quhair ther wes ane verie great confluence of all ranks of people to heare old Mr. John Row, quho, for many zeares befor, wes not permitted to preach in Edinburgh."[2]

The next stage in the evolution of the drama was the signing, on 28th February 1638, of the National Covenant within the walls of the Church of the Greyfriars. Unfortunately, tradition, with its usual pertinacity, has greatly altered and obscured the details of that historic incident; and it is mainly through the recent discovery of an early portion of Wariston's *Diary* that the true facts have been revealed. Dr. Hay Fleming, the discoverer of that portion, and an acknowledged authority on the Covenanting period, has, at my special request, written for us the true account of the proceedings of that eventful day—to be found in the succeeding chapter, No. VIII.

[1] Wariston's *Diary*, p. 267.   [2] Row's *History* (Maitland Club), i. p. 255.

Halt passenger take heed q' thou dost see
This tomb doth shew for q' some men did die
Here lyes interr'd y dust of these who stood
Gainst perjury resisting unto blood
Adhering to the Covenants and Laws
Establishing the same which was the Cause:
Then lives were sacrific'd unto the Lust
Of Prelatist's abjur'd though here their dust.
Ly's mixt with murderers and other crew
Whom justice did justly to death pursue.
But as for thir in them no cause was found
Worthy of death but only they were found
Constant and stedfast Zealous wittnessing
For the prerogatives of CHRIST their king
Which truth's were seal'd by famous Guthri's
                          head
And all along to Master Ranwick's blood
They did endure the wrath of enemies
Reproaches torments deaths and injuries
But yet they're these who from such trobls came
And now triumph in glory with the LAMB

From may 27th 1661 that the noble Marquess of
Argyle suffered to the 17th of febr 1688 that Mr
Iames Ranwick suffer.d were execut at Edin-
burg about an hundered of Noblemen Gent
lmen Ministers & others noble martyres for
IESUS CHRIST: the most part of them ly
This Tomb was here. Erected. Anno 1706

ORIGINAL STONE OF THE MARTYRS' MONUMENT. ERECTED 1706. REMOVED 1771.
Now preserved in the Edinburgh City Museum.

CHURCH OF THE GREYFRIARS IN 1647.
From Drawing by Gordon of Rothiemay (enlarged).

VIII

THE SUBSCRIBING OF THE NATIONAL COVENANT IN 1638

BY D. HAY FLEMING, LL.D.

The earliest of the nineteenth-century detailed accounts of the subscribing of the National Covenant in the spring of 1638, are, so far as I know, those written by Robert Chambers and the Rev. John Aiton of Dolphinton. The one by Chambers is in his *History of the Rebellions in Scotland under the Marquis of Montrose and others,* published in 1828 (i. 92–97); and the other, by Aiton, is in his *Life and Times of Alexander Henderson,* published in 1836 (pp. 250–260). These accounts have apparently influenced the later ones, and are thus to some extent responsible for the current conception. The authorities cited by Chambers are *Straloch's MS.,* Advocates' Library; Guthry's *Memoirs;* and Rothes' *Relation.* Of these three, when Chambers wrote, only one had been published, namely,

Guthry's *Memoirs*, which had gone through three editions, respectively issued in 1702, 1747, and 1748.   Rothes' *Relation* was subsequently printed for the Bannatyne Club in 1830; and the Spalding Club, in 1841, published Gordon's *History of Scots Affairs*, fragments of which had been copied into James Man's *Historical Collections*, "generally quoted under the name of the 'Straloch MS.,' but apparently upon no better authority than that of the title on the backs of the volumes."

Both Chambers's account and Aiton's are incorrect in some of their details.   The precise date when the Covenant was signed in the Greyfriars' Church has been given as the 1st of March by such competent modern historians as Malcolm Laing (*History of Scotland*, 1800, i. 136), George Cook (*History of the Church of Scotland*, 1815, ii. 416, 417), the elder M'Crie (*Miscellaneous Writings*, p. 17), and the younger M'Crie (*Story of the Scottish Church*, 1875, p. 145). They were misled on this point by Bishop Guthry, William Row, and John Livingstone.   Chambers and Aiton were saved from this error by Rothes' *Relation*; but while giving the correct date, Wednesday, 28th February, on which it was first signed in the Greyfriars' Church, they add that, later on the same day, it was taken out to the churchyard, laid on a flat gravestone, and there signed by a vast number of people.   That it was subscribed in the churchyard as well as in the church was distinctly asserted by George Crawfurd in 1726 (*Lives and Characters of the Officers of the Crown and of the State in Scotland*, i. 186).   His words are :—

"The Covenant in this sense was first publickly read and subscribed in the Gray-frier's Church and Churchyard at Edinburgh, the 1st of March 1638, by a numerous assembly, with great joy and shouting."

The only authority he cites in support of this statement

is Bishop Guthry's *Memoirs*. The relative passage in these *Memoirs* (1702, p. 30), runs thus :—

" And so upon the 1st of March 1638, they being all assembled in the Gray-Friers Church and Churchyard, the Covenant (having been prepared before hand) was publickly read, and subscrib'd by them all with much joy and shouting."

While Guthry here asserts that the Covenanters were assembled in the church and churchyard, he does not say explicitly whether the Covenant was read and subscribed in the church or churchyard or in both. It may be inferred from his statement that it was read in both and subscribed in both ; and yet he might only mean that it was read in the church, and that the people who were in the church-yard went into the church in batches to sign. Robert Chambers seems to be the first writer to assert that a gravestone was used on the occasion. He says :—

" When it [*i.e.* the Covenant] had taken the round of the whole church, it was handed out to the immense multi-tude which had collected in the churchyard ; and there being received with no less rapture than in the church, it was laid upon one of the flat monuments so thickly scattered around, and subscribed by all who could get near it. It is said by one of the contemporary chroniclers so often quoted, to have been a most impressive sight, when the Covenant was read to this vast crowd, to see thousands of faces and hands at once held up to heaven in token of assent, while devout aspirations burst from every lip, and tears of holy joy distilled from every eye."

Not being given by Chambers within inverted commas, the last sentence may be regarded as his summary or paraphrase of the contemporary chronicler whose name he does not mention. There is no such passage in any of the works which he cites as his authorities for this chapter ;

H

but among the authorities he cites for a previous chapter is Livingstone's *Autobiography* in the Wodrow MSS., Advocates' Library. That autobiography, which had been printed in 1754, has, since Chambers wrote, been published from the Wodrow MSS. by the Wodrow Society, and contains (*Select Biographies*, i. 160) this statement :—

" I was present at Lanerk and at severall other paroches, when, on ane Sabbath after the forenoon sermon, the Covenant was read and sworn, and may truely say that in all my life, except one day in the church of Shotts, I never saw such motions from the Spirit of God ; all the people generally and most willingly concurring, where I have seen above 1000 persons all at once lifting up their hands, and the tears dropping from their eyes."

This may be the statement which Chambers paraphrased ; but it relates to Lanark and other parishes, not to Edinburgh ; to subscribing on the Sabbath, not on a weekday.

Of the accounts written by contemporaries, one of the fullest is by James Gordon, parson of Rothiemay, who was born about 1615. Apparently he was not in Edinburgh when the Covenant was subscribed there, and consequently he was dependent on the testimony of others. As he says that " most of thes passages are fresh in the memoryes of many yet living," it is obvious that he did not write his account until a considerable period had elapsed. As some of his details were not recorded by his contemporaries, the more important parts of his version (as printed for the Spalding Club, in his *History of Scots Affairs*, i. 43–45) may be quoted :—

" The Covenant, which was the grand result and conclusione of the Tables[1] at ther meeting in February, 1638, was no sooner agreed upon but instantly it was begunne

---

[1] The representative committees of the Covenanters at that time were called *tables*.

to be subscrybed in Edinburgh first.[1]   And the churche
chosne out for that solemnitye was the Gray Freers Churche
in Edinburgh ; wher, after it had been reade over publickly
and a long speeche had been made by the Lord Lowdone
in commendatione therof, Mr. Alexander Henderson seconded him with a prayer, and then all fell to sweare and
subscrybe, some of the nobilitye leading the way.   The
first (as I am credibly informed) was Johne Gordon, Earle
of Sutherlande, and the next was Sir Andrew Murrey,
Lord Balvard, minister at Ebdy, in Fyfe : two noblemen
who, out of zeale to ther professione, without any by ende,
thought it ane happinesse to be amongst the first subscribents and swearers to the Covenant.   After them, all
that wer present ranne to the subscriptione of it, and then
through the rest of the cittye it went, evry one contesting
who might be first ; and others, without furder examina-
tion or questioning the articles therof, following the example
of others, women, young people, and servant maides, did
sweare and hold upp ther handes to the Covenant.   All
who wer present at Edinburgh at that meeting in the
moneth of Februarye, subscrybed and swore to the Cove-
nante befor they went from thence ; and, at ther parting,
ministers, and noblemen, and gentlemen, who wer weal
affected to the cause, carryd coppyes therof along with
them, or caused them to be wryttne out after ther returne
to ther severall paroshines and counteys of Scotland.
Which coppyes wer ordinarly wryttne upon great skinnes
of parchement (for which cause at that tyme, in a wryttne

[1] In a footnote, Rothiemay says : " It beganne to be subscrybed in
March.   See ther protestation in July, 1638."   That protestation (*Large
Declaration*, 1639, p. 100) contains the words : " In the moneth of March . . .
wee were necessitate to renew the Nationall Covenant of this Kirk and Kingdome."
These words, however, do not imply that the subscribing began in March.
The protestation runs in the names of the " noblemen, barons, gentlemen,
burgesses, ministers, and commons " ; and though the nobles, barons, and
gentry signed on the 28th of February, the burgesses, ministers, and commons
had no opportunity of doing so until March.   In December of that year, the
General Assembly declared (*Acts of Assembly*, Church Law Society ed., pp. 18, 31)
that the Covenant was renewed in February.   According to Livingstone (*Select
Biographies*, i. 159), " they did, in the beginning of March, renew the National
Covenant."

pasqwell, the Covenant was termed, *The Constellatione upon the backe of Aries*). And such as tooke coppyes along with them for to be subscrybed, caused ordinarly such as had sworne or underwrytne ther names alreadye (if they were noblemen or ministers of note), for to sett too their hands anew to the several coppyes, that, wher themselves could not be present to invitte others, ther hand wrytte might be ther proxye. To sett off the great solemnity of this tacking the Covenant with the greater grace, there was one Mr. Thomas Abernetthye (a new convert from Popery, who laitly had been a seminary priest) *reserved.*[1] This Mr. Thomas Abernetthye was brought in publicke by Mr. Andrew Ramsey and a preface made concerning him, who was standing by in secular apperrall ; who afterwards seconded Mr. Andrew Ramsey his discourse, and declared to the people how farr he had been missledd, and what great attemptes the Pope and his conclave had been and was acting against Scotland, and did as yet continew to acte ; and now shewed, with teares, that he was a lost sheepe, and begged for to have the licence to subscrybe the Covenant, which was granted, and he was surounded by the crowde of the devouter sexe present.[2] . . .

[1] *Reserved* is probably a slip for *received.*

[2] According to John Row of Aberdeen (Row's *History*, Wodrow Society, p. 499), Abernethie "was admitted to the Covenant, and publictlie, August 24, in the Great Kirk of Edinburgh." Following Row unsuspectingly, the Rev. Sir James Cameron Lees identified "the Great Kirk" as St. Giles (*St. Giles', Edinburgh*, 1889, p. 214) ; but Sir Thomas Hope (*Diary*, Bannatyne Club, p. 76) says that he was "ressavit in the Greyfreir Kirk" ; and Wariston (*Diary*, 1911, p. 376) says "in the Grayfreires." Hope and Wariston are corroborated by Abernethie himself, in his *Abjuration of Poperie*, by the "sometime Jesuite, but now penitent sinner, and an unworthie member of the true Reformed Church of God in Scotland," which was printed in 1638, and bears to have been made "at Edinburgh, in the Grayfrier Church, the 24 of August 1638." Row gives the 24th of August as the date ; Hope and Wariston give Thursday, the 23rd. Baillie (*Letters and Journals*, i. 102) says that it was on a Thursday ; and, in 1638, the 23rd of August fell on a Thursday. That the 24th on Abernethie's title-page is not a misprint, is shown by his reference to St. Bartholomew's day in his opening paragraph. Ramsay's sermon "at the receiving of Mr. Thomas Abernethie, sometime Jesuite, into the societie of the truely reformed Church of Scotland," was also printed in 1638 ; but it gives neither the date when, nor the church where, it was preached.

" The moneths of February, March, and Apryle, were mostlye spent in subscrybing the Covenant ; and all that tyme, and some whyle therafter, in purchassing[1] handes therunto. The greater that the number of subscribents grew, the mor imperiouse they wer in exacting subscriptiones from others who refoosed to subscrybe ; so that by degrees they proceeded to contumelys and exposing of many to injuryes and reproaches, and som wer threatned and beatne who durst refoose, specially in greatest cittyes (as lyckwayes in other smaller townes), namely, at Edinburgh, Saint Andrews, Glasgow, Lanerke, and many other places. Gentlemen and noblemen carryd coppyes of it about in ther portmantles and pocketts, reqwyring subscriptiones therunto, and usinge ther utmost endeavours with ther freendes in private for to subscrybe. It was subscrybed publickly in churches, ministers exhorting ther people therunto. It was also subscrybed and sworne privattly. All had power to tacke the oathe, and wer licenced and welcome to come in, and any that pleased had power and licence for to carye the Covenant about with him, and give the oathe to such as wer willinge to subscrybe and sweare. And such was the zeale of many subscribents, that, for a whyle, many subscrybed with teares on ther cheekes, and it is constantly reported that some did draw ther owne blood and used it in place of inke to underwrytte ther names. Such ministers as spocke most for it wer heard so passionatly and with such freqwencye, that churches could not containe ther hearers in cittyes."

Chambers unhesitatingly adopted Rothiemay's report regarding the Earl of Sutherland, and ventured to describe him as " a nobleman venerable for his excellent domestic character."[2] Aiton referred to him simply as " the venerable Earl of Sutherland." This was much too commonplace

[1] *Purchasing*, that is, *procuring*.

[2] Rothiemay seems to be the only contemporary who refers to Sutherland as the first to sign the Covenant. Of that he was " credibly informed." Sutherland's name heads the list of nobles in a petition against the Service Book and the Book of Canons (*Maitland Miscellany*, ii. 413).

for Hetherington, who, with Aiton before him, speaks (*History of the Church of Scotland*, 7th ed. i. 300) of " an aged nobleman, the venerable Earl of Sutherland," stepping " slowly and reverentially forward," and subscribing " with throbbing heart and trembling hand." As John, thirteenth Earl of Sutherland, was born on the 9th of March 1609 (Fraser's *Sutherland Book*, i. 209), he was barely twenty-nine years of age on the 28th of February 1638. Andrew Murray, the minister of Abdie, had been knighted in 1633, but was not created Lord Balvaird until 1641. It is note-worthy that the parson of Rothiemay, while emphatically affirming that the Covenant was subscribed in the Grey-friars' Church, does not even mention the churchyard. The testimony of William Row of Ceres, in the supplement to his father-in-law's autobiography (*Blair's Life*, Wodrow Society, p. 155), is to the same effect :—

" They did in March 1638, very solemnly in the Grey-friars' Kirk in Edinburgh, renew that National Covenant, and thereafter throughout the kingdom most solemnly."

In a pamphlet printed in 1638, entitled *A Short Relation of the State of the Kirk of Scotland*, by " an hearty well-wisher to both Kingdomes," neither the church nor the churchyard is mentioned :—

" This Covenant was subscribed by many thousands in Februarie last, yea in a very short time, by almost the whole kingdome. It was publickly read and sworne in most kirks, with great motion, prayers, and teares, all professing repentance for their sinnes, specially for their breach of Covenant to God in suffering the puritie of his worship to bee thus tainted."

There is, in the Church of Scotland Library, a manu-script volume in a seventeenth-century hand, entitled *The Historie of Church and State of Scotland, from the begininge of King Charles the First his raigne untill the end of the yeare of our Lord 1646.* The author, who was a contemporary, says (p. 29) :—

" In the moneth of Feberuary 1638 was the Covenant renewed, and a oath for mutuall defence of one annother, in defence of religion and liberty of the kingdome, the King's royall person and honnour, annexed thereto ; and the copie thereof sent through all the parishes of the kingdome to be subscribed ; and it was gladlie welcomed by manie thousands in the land ; some refuseinge at first, haveinge their owne doubts, and was loath to subscrive till they gave satisfactione to their consciences ; others, haveing dependence one bishopps, held off, because they saw the roote of that tree aimed at to be plucked up ; and all Papists refused it."

My friend, the Rev. John Sturrock, owns a manuscript history, which is also in a seventeenth-century hand, and which is entitled, *The Rise, Reigne and Ruine of the Scottish Prelats once and againe.* According to it :—

" Thus the Covenant is subscribed by all those who were then present at Edinburgh in February 1638 ; and copies thereof are sent to such as were absent, that all such as loved the puritie of religion might signe the same ; and it was so weell accepted that, befor the end of Aprile, he was not accownted a professor of the reformed religion who did not subscribe the same."

Similarly, no particular church is named by John Row of Aberdeen, in his *Handfull of Goat's Haire for the furthering of the building of the Tabernacle* (Row's *History*, Wodrow Society, p. 489) :—

" In the end of February, the Covenant was drawen up, by commune consent of all the commissioners, was read in all the pulpitts of Edinburgh, and in a few dayes was sworne and subscryved almost by all, onlie Aberdeen excepted."

All the foregoing accounts are surpassed in importance by that given in Rothes' *Relation* (p. 70) :—

" Bishops had their emissaries also, who came out, lyke Joab to Abner, under fair pretences, affirmeing they wer now so desyreous of peace to the Churche and countrey, as they wold become intercessours to his Majestie for removeing the Service-book and Canons, and for restraineing the High Commissione, yea wold undertake to obtaine it : they wold gratifie the supplicants one crop so they might keip the inheritance. Bot all resolved to stop their ears at these charmes ; and as they wer not gathered mutinouslie by one or a few men, bot by God and a good cause, so did all perceave his continuing conduct by moveing a conjunct motione from the nobilitie, gentrie, burgesses, and ministers, of renueing that same Covenant subscribed by our ancestours, with such additions as the corruptiones of this tyme necessarilie requyred to be joyned, and such Acts of Parliament as was against Poperie and in favours of the true religione. This, being drawen, was revised and corrected by divers learned ministers, and subscribed by many thousands[1] of the nobilitie and gentrie, at the Grayfreir Kirk, on Wedinsday the last of February ; and by many hundreths of ministers, on Thursday the first of Marche, and by many of the burrowes ; with such mutuall contentment and joy as these, who, haveing long befor bein outlawes and rebells, ar admitted againe in covenant with God, and advowe their obedience to him as their protectour, who can and will safe them from these present and all suche evills ; herby also their hearts ar stronglie united one to another."

After making this statement, the writer goes back in

[1] *Thousands* is obviously a mistake here. I have examined the passage in the three oldest MS. copies of the work in the Advocates' Library, and found that this mistake occurs in them all. The passage has been copied into the so-called "Straloch MS." (35, 4. 3, vol. i. b. 2, par. 39) as a footnote, and there it also reads *thousands*. As will be subsequently seen, the nobles began to subscribe at four o'clock in the afternoon, and were followed by the barons, none of whom signed after eight o'clock. As there was then only one principal copy, it was manifestly impossible for thousands to sign in four hours.

his narrative to Friday, the 23rd of February; and recounts what was done day by day. On that Friday (p. 71), "Mr. Alexander Hendersone, minister, and Mr. Archibald Johnestone, advocate, wer appoynted to draw up the Confessione of Faith, with sic additiones as the change of tymes, and the present occasione, requyred." It is hardly necessary to explain that by the Confession of Faith is meant the Covenant drawn up by John Craig, which was first subscribed in January 1580–81, and frequently afterwards. "Upon Satturday" (p. 71), "the noblemen did meit againe, wher Rothes, Loudon, Balmerinoche, wer appoynted to revise what Mr. Hendersone and Mr. Johnstone had done." On the morning of Monday, the 26th of February (p. 72), "the noblemen met againe at Mr. Johne Gallowayes house, wher Mr. Hendersone and Mr. Johnestone shew that it was impossible to gett that which was put upone them ready so soon: desired Rothes, Loudon, Balmerinoche, to revise it againe, and they sould use all expeditione for haveing it ready against Tuysday in the morning." When the nobles met in John Galloway's house on Tuesday (pp. 72–76), "the Confessione of Faith was red, and the additiones which concernes us according to the difference of tyme, with certaine Acts of Parliament establishing the true religione and policie of the Kirk, and favouring our present way." Certain objections were raised and discussed. Rothes, Loudoun, and others then went to "Tailyours' Hall," to meet the ministers who were assembled there. Deeming it expedient that the commissioners of presbyteries should be first spoken to apart, "they went into the summer-house in the yaird," where the draft was read, discussed, and in one passage amended. Returning to the other ministers, who numbered between two and three hundred, the amended draft was read and received "with verrie great heartines" by almost all. Then comes the eventful 28th of February (pp. 76–79):—

I

"Upon Wedinsday morning, about half eight, Rothes and Loudon come wher the commissioners of barrons wer mett at Mr. Johne Gallowayes house. . . . It was agreed that all the rest of the barrons and gentilmen, that wer in toune, sould meitt in the Greyfreer Kirk be tuo hours in the efternoone, wher Rothes and Loudon sould meitt with them.

"Being mett, and prayer said by Mr. Alexander Hendersone, verrie powerfullie and pertinentlie to the purpose in hand of renueing the Covenant, Loudon spoke as of befoir to the commissioners of barrons,[1] adding, that the nobilitie, ministers, and commissioners of shires and burrowes, had agreed to this forme which was to be red to them, wherin they took God to witnes they intendit nothing to the dishonour of God or diminutione of the King's honour, and wished they might perishe who myndit other wayes. Efter the reading the draught by Mr. Archibald Johnestone, out of a fair parchment above an ellne in squair, these who had any doubts wer desyred by Rothes, if they wer of the south and west countrey, to go to the west end of the kirk, wher Loudon and Mr. David Dick [better known now as David Dickson] wold attend them; if they wer of the Lothians and on the north side of Forth, to go to the east end of the kirk, wher he and Mr. Alexander Hendersone sould attend them for giveing satisfactione to them. Few came, and those few proponed a few doubts, which wer resolved. The noblemen came thither at four hours and subscryved. The barrons subscryved efter them, so many as could subscryve that night, whill it was neir eight. . . .

"Upon Thursday, the first of March, Rothes, Lindsay,

---

[1] That morning, in John Galloway's house, Loudoun had urged that, as the adversaries had tried to weaken them by division, so they should use all lawful means to keep themselves together in their common cause; that the example of their predecessors gave them a precedent how to bind themselves together, for maintenance of the true religion and the King's honour and authority; that the reading of the document would give them fuller information; that it had been first submitted to the ministers, because much of it was theological; that they had assented to it; and that now it was submitted to the barons, that they might state any material doubts they might have.

and Loudon, and sum of them, went down to Tailyours'
Hall, wher the ministers mett ; and becaus sum wer come
to toune since Tuysday last who had sum doubts, efter
that they who had bein formerlie resolved wer entered to
subscryve, the noblemen went with these others to the
yaird, and resolved their doubts ; so that towards thrie
hundred ministers subscryved that night. That day the
commissioners of burrowes subscryved also."

On Friday, the 2nd of March (pp. 79, 80), it was resolved
that those "ministers, who have not mett nor subscryved,
and will practise conformitie," should be " exhorted and
invited to do otherways ; and, if they wold not, to be
discountenanced and dishaunted by them all, and all they
could persuade." And on the same day :—

" It was concludit, that a copie of the Confessione
[*i.e.* of the Covenant] sould be provydit for ilk shire,
balzierie, stewardrie, or distinct judicatorie, wherat may
be all the hands of the principall persons in the saids circuits,
and a particular one to be drawne for ilk parosche within
the said judicatories, wherat may be all the hands of the
persons in the said parosche that ar admitted to the sacrament ; and these who cannot subscryve themselves, that
a couple of nottars shall subscryve for them."

It is very suggestive that, in this contemporary and
detailed account the churchyard of Greyfriars is not once
mentioned. No room is left for doubt that it was agreed
that the barons and gentlemen (not the populace) should
meet " in the Greyfreer Kirk," by two o'clock in the afternoon of Wednesday, the 28th of February ; that, being
met, Henderson prayed, Loudoun spoke, and Archibald
Johnston read the Covenant " out of a fair parchment,"
above an ell square ; that an opportunity was given to
those who had doubts to express them ; that, at four
o'clock, the nobles came and subscribed ; and that the
barons subscribed after them, " so many as could subscryve

that night," until it was nearly eight o'clock. Apparently
no others signed that day.[1] Next day, Rothes, Lindsay,
Loudoun, and others, went to the Tailors' Hall to meet the
ministers; and after those of them who had been formerly
satisfied had begun to subscribe, Rothes and the other
nobles went " to the yaird " (evidently the garden of the
Tailors' Hall [2]) with the doubting ones who had come to
town since Tuesday, and cleared up their difficulties. By
night nearly three hundred ministers had subscribed. The
commissioners of burghs also signed that day.

So far then as Rothes' *Relation* shows, the Covenant
was only signed on the 28th of February and the 1st of
March, by nobles, barons, ministers, and commissioners of
burghs, in Greyfriars' Church and the Tailors' Hall, and
nowhere by the populace. This is pretty strong evidence,
though mainly negative, that, to begin with, the Covenant
was neither sworn nor subscribed by the people in the
Greyfriars' Churchyard. Taken by itself, this evidence
would not be strong enough to overthrow any clear contemporary statement to the contrary; but, so far as I
know, there is none such. Before considering the precise
nature and value of Bishop Guthry's statement, it may
be well to look at the valuable evidence of Archibald
Johnston (afterwards Lord Wariston) which was not published until May 1911. As secretary of the Scottish History
Society, I read in August 1908, in the original MS., the
following passages, which staggered my belief in the churchyard subscription; and subsequent investigation has confirmed my doubts. Here the passages are quoted from
the printed volume, so admirably edited by Sir George

---

[1] Had New Style been adopted in Scotland then, that day would have been
reckoned as the 10th of March; but, even on the 10th of March, as we reckon,
artificial light must have been used in the church shortly after six o'clock.

[2] The Tailors' Hall in the Cowgate is illustrated and described in Sir Daniel
Wilson's *Memorials of Edinburgh in the Olden Time*, 1891, ii. 144–146.

M. Paul (*Diary of Sir Archibald Johnston of Wariston,
1632–1639*, pp. **318–323**) :—

"Upon Fraday, 23 Feb. . . . the insupportable burden
of drauing up the Band, quherby al sould be linked together
after subscryving of the Confession of Fayth, was laid
upon my weak schoulders, so that afternoone, after manifold
thanks for quhat grounds he had put in my mynd foranoone, and for thair happie succes, I prayed on my knees
earnestly the Lord to assist, direct, infuse, and guide immediatly by his Sprit my heart, hand, tounge, and pen,
in the framing and forming thairof in that maner quhilk
might tend most to his glorie, this churche's wealfaire,
the standing of our religion, laues, liberties, and comon-
wealth, our stricter union with him and amongst ourselves, the greater opposition to idolatrie and al uther
innovations, the instruction of posteritie and my auin
salvation through Chryst Jesus, *in cujus nomine incipio*. . . .
Thairafter Mr. Alexander Henderson, haiving sayd a pithie
schort prayer for God's direction, and I fell to the Band,
quhairof we scrolled the narrative.

"On Saturday morning, after incalling the naime of
God, on quhom is my only trust fixed, I fell to the drauing
out the main points out of the Acts of Parliament to be
put in the Band. Lord, assiste for Chryst saik. Again
tuo hours I ended that task ; and quhyle I was going to
apply it, I was sent for, and read them to Rothes, Laudin,
Balmerino, quho comanded me to compendize them.

"On Sunday, 25, being keiped as ane fast and humilia-
tion for our former breatches of the Covenant, and as ane
praeparation to the renovation thairof and to the manifold
important consultations at this great meiting, . . . About
six hours in the morning thou [1] epitomized som of thy
Acts ; [2] thou got som tears in the morning in thy familie,
and ane great earnestnes at night, but noe tears in thy
retyring.

"On Mononday morning I, after requeisting the Lord to

---

[1] Wariston very often thus addresses his soul.

[2] That is, the Acts of Parliament selected for insertion in the Covenant.

rinse the vessel and then to poure in the liquor of his heievinly directions to moderat, assist, direct the consultations, and particularly about the Band, *in nomine Domini mei incipio.* Thairafter began, nyn hours. I, after ane earnest prayer to the Lord to red my feet quhilk was so intangled in the ordoring of my confused thoughts, I got by God's great assistance al digested in three heads, quhilk was approvin by the Committe apoynted to reveiu them. At night we sau apearance of great opposition amongst the ministerie and barons, and from the great grandies of lauers, quherwith som was dasched, my fearful conjectures was increassed ; yet my desyre and resolution for the Band was by the sam opposition augmented.

"On Tuesday, 27 Feb., I was taiken out befor I got myselth weal recomended to God, greu in desyre of the Band for God's glorie ever as I sau or heard of any appearance of fear. I read Confession, Acts of Parlim., and Band to the nobles, be quhom tuo words wer chainged. Afternoon with great fears we went to the ministerie ; and, after tuo other alterations and ane discussion of al objections, we got it approvin first be the commissioners [of presbyteries], then be the whol ministerie except on [*i.e.* one] *non liquet* becaus of his oath to the bischop to practise perpetualy. . . . In the meantyme, being advertised by John Kelou of Sanders Couper's speetches and threats eyther to haive my lyfe or I to haive his, I was never dasched at the matter, bot went on to gar wryte the Band in parchment, casting my lyfe this way or that way in the hands of my God, the praeserver and faithful redeemer both of my saul and body through Chryst Jesus the God of my salvation.

"Upon Wedensday, 28 Februar, that glorious mariage day of the Kingdome with God, I was al foranoone with the commissioners of the barons, quho, after long reasoning upon Perth Articles,[1] did al appreive except the Laird of

---

[1] By a majority, a General Assembly, held at Perth in 1618, agreed to five articles, which were ratified by Parliament in 1621, and were known as "the Articles of Perth." By these, (1) kneeling at the Lord's Supper was approved; (2) ministers were to dispense that sacrament in private houses to those suffering

Ethie; so the burroues. The noblemen haiving apoynted the body of the gentrie to meit at tuo hours in the Gray-frear Kirk to hear bot copyes of it read and to aunsuear objections, I propons and resolves to haive the principal ready in parchment in al hazards, that, in cais of approbation, it might be presently subscryved. I mett al the gentlemen in on [i.e. one] troupe going up the cassie to the Kirk. I resolved to read and did read the parchment itselth publikly, quhilk, after som feu doubts of som, was approvin; and after ane divine prayer, most fit for the tyme and present purpose, maid be Mr. Alexander Henderson, the Covenant was subscryved first be the noblemen and barons al that night til 8 at night.

"On Foorsday morning I had wryting in the night foor principal copyes in parchment; at nyn hours it was subscryved be al the ministerie; at tuo hours be the burroues.

"On Frayday, in the College Kirk, after ane sensible exhortation be Mr. H. Rollok, taiken from 4 v. 3 c. Jer., and Samson's mother's aunsuer to Manoah, and ane pithie prayer forcing the to tears, thou read it publikly befor the people of Edinburgh, quho presently fell to the subscryving of it al that day and the morrou."

Like Rothes, Wariston does not mention Greyfriars' Churchyard; and he confirms Rothes' statements that it was in the church that the barons and gentlemen ("the body of the gentrie") met at two o'clock on Wednesday, the 28th of February, and subscribed; and that the ministers and (commissioners of) burghs signed next day. Rothes makes the subscribing on Wednesday go on till "neir eight" at night, and Wariston says "til 8 at night." Like Rothes, Wariston says nothing about the populace signing on either of these days; and his explana-

from infirmity or from long or deadly disease; (3) ministers were to baptize children in private houses in cases of great need; (4) ministers were, under pain of the bishop's censure, to catechise all children of eight years of age, and the children were to be presented to the bishop for his blessing; and (5) ministers were ordered to commemorate Christ's birth, passion, resurrection, ascension, and the sending down of the Holy Ghost.

tion, that he resolved "to haive the principal ready in parchment in al hazards, that, in cais of approbation, it might be presently subscryved," implies that those who assembled in the church that afternoon did not expect to have the opportunity of subscribing then. Moreover, he states that "the people of Edinburgh" subscribed on the Friday and Saturday, not in the Greyfriars' Church or Churchyard, but "in the College Kirk," that is, Trinity College Kirk, which stood at the foot of Leith Wynd.

Bishop Guthry's account may now be critically examined. As already mentioned, his work was first printed in 1702. It is entitled: *Memoirs of Henry Guthry, late Bishop of Dunkel, in Scotland: wherein the conspiracies and rebellion against King Charles I. of blessed memory, to the time of the murther of that Monarch, are briefly and faithfully related.* The editor acknowledges that it was not published from the original MS., but "from an authentick copy." The late Bishop Dowden also possessed a MS. copy, which is now in the Chapter House of St. Mary's Cathedral, Edinburgh. I have collated the passage, and, as there are several notable variations, it is herewith subjoined in both versions :—

Printed Edition of 1702.	*Bishop Dowden's MS. Copy.*
" But the noblemen, and the wisest of the ministers, abhorred the motion, and so nothing of that kind was attempted, only having spoken with the treasurer, and commissionated Arthur Airskin of Scotscraig, and Sir William Murray of Pomeis, to renew their declinature at the first diet of Council, the noblemen, and all the rest, (reckoned above 2000) rode straight from Sterling to Edinburgh, there to consult what was next to be done; whereof the issue	" But the noblemen, and wisest of the ministers, abhorred the motione, and so nothing was furthir attempted at that tyme; onlie haveing spoken with the thesaurer and others of the Counsell, and commissionat Arthur Areskine of Scotscraig, and Sir Williame Murray off Polmais, to renew the declinatour at the first dyet of Counsell, the noblemen, and all the rest, (reckoned to be above 1000) rode straight from Stirling to Edenburgh, to consult what was nixt

Printed Edition of 1702—*continued.*

was, that, after some days advisement and consultation with Sir Thomas Hope and other lawyers, they resolv'd upon a Covenant, to be subscribed by all that would join with them.

"And so upon the 1st of March 1638, they being all assembled in the Gray-Friers Church, and Churchyard, the Covenant (having been prepared before hand) was publickly read, and subscrib'd by them all with much joy and shouting.

"The Archbishop of St. Andrews being then return'd from Sterling to Edinburgh, when he heard what was done, said, *Now all that we have been doing these* 30 *years past is thrown down at once;*[1] and fearing violence, he presently fled away to London (where the next year he died), so did also such other of the bishops, as knew themselves most ungracious to the people; only four of them stay'd at home, whereof three delivered their persons and fortunes from sufferings, by their solemn recantations; those were Mr. Alexander Ramsey, Bishop of Dunkeld, Mr. George Graham, Bishop of Orkney, and Mr. James Fairly, Bishop of Argile; but the fourth, Mr. John Guthry, Bishop of Murray, as he

Bishop Dowden's MS. Copy—continued.

to be done; whairoff the issue was, eftir some dayes advisement and consultatione with Sir Thomas Hope and other lawers, that a Covenant should be subscrived by all that would joyne with them.

"And so upon the first of March 1638 they being all assembled in the Grayfriers Churchyaird, the Covenant being prepared beforhand was publictly red and subscrived by them all with much joy and shouting.

"The Archbishop of St. Andrews being returned to Edinburgh from Stirling, when he heard what was done, said, *Now all that we have been building these* 30 *yeires past is throughlie down at once*; and fearing violence presentlie fled to London (whair the nixt yeir he died). So did also such other of the bishopes as knew themselvs to be most ungracious to the people. Onlie four of them stayed at home, wheroff thrie delivered both ther persons and fortuns from suffering by ther solemne recantationes. These ar Mr. Alexander Lindsay, Bishop of Dunkeld, Mr. George Græme, Bishop of Orknay, and Mr. James Fairlie, Bishop of Argyle. But the fourt, Mr. John Guthrie, Bishop of Murray, as he choosed not to flie, so upon no termes would

[1] The archbishop's opinion is phrased somewhat differently in Matthew Crawfurd's MS. *History of the Church of Scotland* (vol. i. part ii. p. 125): "It wes said that, when first the Covenant wes subscribed, that Archbishop Spotswood, understanding that a great number of people wer in the Grayfrier Church in Edinburgh, sent to enquire what the matter wes; and being informed that the noblemen and others were renewing the Covenant, he said, We have been making a tub these fourty years, and now the bottome thereof is fallen out." This MS. is in the Church of Scotland Library.

K

Printed Edition of 1702—continued.

chose not to flee, so upon no terms would he recant, but patiently endured excommunication, imprisonment, and other sufferings, and in the midst of them stood to the justification of Episcopal government until his death.

"Many copies of the Covenant were sent through the country to the several presbyteries, burroughs, and parishes, to be subscribed; which was every where done with joy, except in the North parts, where many oppos'd it."

Bishop Dowden's MS. Copy—continued.

he recant; but patiently indured excommunicatione, imprisonment, and other sufferings, and in the midst of them stood to the justification of Episcopall government to his death, etc.

"Many copies of the Covenant wer sent through the countrey to severall presbitries, burghs, and paroches, to be subscrived, which was evrie wher done with joy except in the North pairts wher many opposed it."

Bishop Dowden's MS. is not a copy of the printed book. This is indicated by some of the variations in the passage just quoted. The figure 1 of that period, as frequently written, might easily be mistaken by a careless or inexperienced transcriber for 2; but the printed 2 could not be mistaken for 1. And so, in the first paragraph, 1000 is probably correct, and 2000 wrong. Again, in the third paragraph, the print is certainly wrong in giving *Ramsey* as the surname of the Bishop of Dunkeld, and the MS. is undoubtedly right in giving it as *Lindsay*. Besides, the handwriting of the MS. seems to me to belong to the latter part of the seventeenth century, and therefore to be earlier than the print. George Crawfurd, in his *Life of Bishop Guthry*, prefixed to the 1748 edition of the *Memoirs*, says that he " was generally esteemed a wise man, moderate in his temper, regular and exemplary in the whole course of his life." On the other hand, two-and-forty years before, Principal Forrester had described him as one " who loved always to swim with the stream and court the rising sun," as one who, at the time of the bishops' downfall, had denounced the prelates in unmeasured language, and after the Restoration had been one of the readiest to conform

(*Review and Consideration of two late Pamphlets*, 1706, pp. 35, 36). For the present inquiry, it matters little whether Crawfurd or Forrester was right in their estimates of Guthry's character. He could have no object to serve in misrepresenting the place where the Covenant was first signed. His knowledge, however, may have been inferior to that of Rothes and Wariston, for it is uncertain whether he was present, whereas they both took a leading part on the occasion. Their statements, moreover, were committed to writing almost immediately, whereas his, apparently, not until many years afterwards.[1]

The most noticeable discrepancy between the printed *Memoirs* and Bishop Dowden's MS. quoted above, is that while the one says that the Covenanters were " assembled in the Grayfriers' Church and Churchyard," the other says that they were " assembled in the Grayfriers' Churchyard," thus ignoring the church. If the print is correct the subscriptions may have been adhibited both in the church and churchyard, though not necessarily so ; if the MS. is correct, in the churchyard alone. The print does not agree with Rothes and Wariston ; the MS. contradicts them, and also contradicts both Rothiemay and William Row.

There is another point which must not be overlooked. Despite the variations of the print and the MS., the substance of the first paragraph of the quotation from Bishop Guthry is the same in both. Those who assembled in the Grey-

---

[1] Rothes' account was drawn up and revised between the 3rd and 5th of March (*Relation*, p. 81). Some portions at least of Wariston's *Diary* were written up day by day (*e.g.* see pp. 352, 353). Guthry refers parenthetically (*Memoirs*, p. 47) to the death of Sir William Dick, who is known (*Acts of Parliament of Scotland*, vi. part ii. p. 756) to have been alive in 1654. Writing on the 13th of February 1703, Bishop Paterson says: " I am sorrie such Memoirs sould ever been written, much more that ever they sould have been printed, and most of all that they sould have a bishop for their author " (*Hamilton Manuscripts*, Hist. MSS. Commission, p. 199). " It was then generally belived that the edition of Bishop Guthry was much altered from the bishop's papers, by the influence of the gentlmen of Oxford who had the publishing of Clarendon in their hands " (Wodrow's *Analecta*, Maitland Club, iv. 299).

friars were not the populace of Edinburgh, but the noblemen and others who had ridden from Stirling to Edinburgh; and so the current accounts of "the immense multitude which had collected in the churchyard" find no support in Bishop Guthry's statement. If the estimated number given in the MS. is correct, those present would have little difficulty in finding room inside the church, which at that time had no pews.

When George Crawfurd's interpretation of Guthry's statement was accepted, the idea of the flat (or table) tombstone would soon suggest itself; and when that idea became common, tradition would select a stone. In this case, tradition was singularly unfortunate and uncritical in pitching upon one which is obviously much too modern.

Hugo Arnot (*History of Edinburgh*, 1779, p. 113), apparently thought that the subscribing in Edinburgh was all done in the same place and on the same occasion :—

" The people being assembled for the purpose in the Greyfriars' Churchyard, the Covenant was solemnly read aloud to them. All ranks and conditions, all ages and sexes, flocked to subscribe it, with that ardour as if they believed the insertion of their names in this parchment scroll did virtually inroll them in the book of life."

With Rothes' *Relation* before him, S. R. Gardiner was much too acute to endorse or accept such an opinion. He acknowledged that the general signature was not described in contemporary accounts, but, as he perceived that the 28th of February and 1st of March were too fully occupied to admit of it on either, he assigned it to the 2nd of March, " though there is no direct evidence about the date." He accepted the tombstone story, however (*History of England from 1603 to 1642*, viii. 333, 334) :—

" On the third day the people of Edinburgh were called

on to attest their devotion to the cause which was represented by the Covenant. Tradition long loved to tell how the honoured parchment, carried back to the Grey Friars, was laid out on a tombstone in the churchyard, whilst weeping multitudes pressed round in numbers too great to be contained in any building. There are moments when the stern Scottish nature breaks out into an enthusiasm less passionate, but more enduring, than the frenzy of a Southern race. As each man and woman stepped forward in turn, with the right hand raised to heaven before the pen was grasped, everyone there present knew that there would be no flinching amongst that band of brothers till their religion was safe from intrusive violence. Modern narrators may well turn their attention to the picturesqueness of the scene, to the dark rocks of the Castle crag over against the Churchyard, and to the earnest faces around. The men of the seventeenth century had no thought to spare for the earth beneath or for the sky above. What they saw was their country's faith trodden under foot, what they felt was the joy of those who had been long led astray, and had now returned to the Shepherd and Bishop of their souls."

Had Gardiner been spared to see Wariston's *Diary*, he would doubtless have been gratified to find that it confirmed his conjecture, that the people of Edinburgh did not subscribe until the 2nd of March; and it is not at all likely that he would have clung to the picturesque story of the Greyfriars' Churchyard and the tombstone.

It must not be supposed, however, that the only opportunity which the people of Edinburgh had to subscribe the Covenant, in 1638, was on Friday and Saturday, the 2nd and 3rd of March, in Trinity College Kirk. In that year the great day of the Covenant in Edinburgh was the 1st of April. Before then, Wariston had told the noblemen of the wonderful scene he had witnessed at Currie, when the Covenant was subscribed there on the 18th of March,[1] and (p. 329) had " heard of the lyk presence of God's Spirit in Craumont, Pans, and many uther congregations "; and, on the 21st of March, he had "read the Confession over to the College, quho subscryved, al the schollers and maisters except Rankin and Broune." On Sabbath, the 1st of April, Wariston heard Mr. Henry Rollock preach in Edinburgh, on Exodus xix. 5, 8, " quhairin he did exceiding weal " :—

" After sermon, and ane intimation for the comunion on the Sunday following and uther three Sundayes, he gart read al the Covenant over ; thairafter he maid ane pithie exhortation anent the present solemne action of suearing to God ; he scheu . . . that the Lord was recalling and reclaiming his people, especyaly this city of Edinburgh. . . . Then he sayd ane verry pithie, pourful, pathetik prayer for the Lord's immediat presence, assistance, and influence upon this congregation, in this most solemne act of worschip ; then he returned to the acceptance of the prodigall son by

---

[1] Mr. John Charteris, the minister of Currie, preached on Gen. xvii. 1, then read the Covenant over as he had done on the previous Sabbath, and explained it. Thereafter, from Neh. x. 28, 29, and 2 Chron. xv. 12–15, he showed his warrant for seeking and theirs for giving the oath. " Yet in al this tyme thair was no motion nor tears in any of the congregation ; bot immediatly thairafter at his lifting up of his hand, and his desyring the congregation to stand up and lift up thair hands and sueare unto the æternal God, and at thair standing up and lifting up thair hands, in the twinkling of ane eye thair fell sutch ane extra-ordinarie influence of God's Sprit upon the whol congregation, melting thair frozen hearts, waltering thair dry cheeks, chainging thair verry countenances, as it was a wonder to seie so visible, sensible, momentaneal a chainge upon al, man and woman, lasse and ladde, pastor and people, that Mr. Jhon, being suffocat almost with his auin tears, and astonisched at the motion of the whol people, sat doune in the pulpit in ane amazement, bot presently rose againe quhen he sau al the people falling doune on thair knees to mourne and pray, and he and thay for ane quarter of ane houre prayed verry sensibly with many sobs, tears, promises, and voues to be thankful and fruitful in tym-coming " (pp. 327, 328). It is no wonder that Wariston regarded this as God's testimony, that the work was " his auin work, his real re-entrie in the Covenant with his people, his acceptance of thair offer, his reservation of ane work of mercie for the congregations of this land."

the kisse of his fayther's mouth. Thairafter he desyred the nobles and al the people, stand up unto the Lord; and first desyred the noblemen, Montrois, Boyd, Laudin, Balmerino, to hold up thair hands and suear be the naime of the living God, and desyred al the people to hold up thairs in the lyk maner; at the quhilk instant of rysing up, and then of holding up thair hands, thair rayse sik a yelloch, sik aboundance of tears, sik a heavenly harmony of sighs and sobbes, universally through all the corners of the churche, as the lyk was never seien nor heard of. The Sprit of the Lord so filled the sanctuary, warmed the affections, melted the hearts, dissolved the eyes of al the people, men and women, poore and noble, as for ane long tyme they stood stil up with thair hands up unto the Lord, til Mr. Hery after he recovered himselth, scairse aible to speak, after ane schort exhortation to thankfulnes and fruitfulnes, closed al up in ane heavenly prayer and prayse, and gart sing the 74 Ps. fra 18 v."

Wariston does not say in which of the Edinburgh churches this took place, although he tells that, in the time of this solemnity, his own heart was like to burst. It is obvious that it was not in a churchyard; and it was not in the Greyfriars,[1] for Wariston (p. 331) proceeds thus :—

"We heard that, in the Grayfrier Kirk, it pleased the Lord both foranoone and afternoone, at the suearing of the Covenant thair, by the lyk motion, to schou the lyk presence of his Sprit. . . . O Edinburgh, O Edinburgh, never

[1] It was probably in Trinity College Kirk, the church of "the North-eist parochin of the burgh of Edinburgh." In the *Register of the Kirk-Session* of that church, Rollock is described, on the 1st of September 1636, as "ane of the ordinar pastors of this parochin"; and, on the 26th of April 1638, as "moderator." As a preparation for renewing the Covenant, it was resolved (Rothes' *Relation*, p. 71) "to have a fast" on Sabbath the 25th of February. "Mr. David Dick[son] was desyred to help Mr. Harie Rollock in the absence of his collegue; and Mr. John Adamsone, Mr. Andro Ramsay his collegue, was desyred to accomodate himselfe to the occasione." Baillie (*Letters*, i. 52) states that Dickson preached in the College Church (that is, Trinity College Kirk) in the forenoon, and Rollock in the afternoon; and that Adamson preached in the Greyfriars in the forenoon, and Ramsay in the afternoon.

forget this first day of Apryle, the gloriousest day that ever thou injoyed!"

Next Sabbath, the 8th of April, "after tuentie yeirs' interruption," the Communion, he says (pp. 334–336), was celebrated purely "in the College and Grayfrears Churche." Mr. Rollock, "scairse aible to speak for cold," preached in the forenoon on Psalm cxxvi. 1, 2; and took "the oath of thos quho had not suorne of befoir, quhairat thair was a verry sensible motion." Because of Rollock's hoarseness, Mr. Robert Blair made all the exhortations; and he preached in the afternoon. Wariston was present, as he also was at Leith on the following Thursday, 12th April (p. 338), where "Mr. Andrew Ramsey haiving read and exponed the Covenant, he gart the people stand up, hold up thair hands, and suear verry solemnely; quhilk God blissed with ane verry sensible motion." On Sabbath the 22nd of April, Wariston accompanied Rothes and Cassillis to Leith (p. 345), "and heard the Covenant read and sau it suorne in the North Kirk of Leyth, Mr. Andreu Forfair haiving teatched 2 v. 3 Revelat."

Writing to William Spang, on the 5th of April, Baillie (*Letters and Journals*, i. 62), after referring to his former letter, says :—

"The great business among us since that tyme hes been, to have that Confession subscryved be all hands; and through all hands almost hes it gone. Of noblemen at home, who are not counsellors or Papists, unto which it was not offered, I think they be within foure or five who hes not subscryved. All the shyres have subscryved, by their commissioners; and all the tounes except Aberdeen, St. Andrews, and Craill; yea, the particular gentlemen, burgesses, and ministers have put to their hands; and the parishes throughout the whole countrey, where the ministers could be persuaded, on a Sabbath day, all have publickly, with ane uplifted hand, man and woman, sworn it."

Although the commissioner for the burgh of St. Andrews had not signed, the people had, for, in the same letter (i. 64), Baillie states that " St. Andrews itself, we hear, for the most part, hes subscryved " ; and, in a later letter (i. 70), he adds : " No a burgesse of St. Andrewes or Dundie refused." The St. Andrews people had not been encouraged by their ministers to sign, and yet they did so with such eagerness and alacrity that Alexander Gladstanes, the minister of the first charge, in denouncing them from the pulpit, said (Wodrow's *Biographical Collections*, Maitland Club, i. 396) " that they hade all runne lyke a companie of mad dogges lett out of a kennell to subscryve the Covenant."

From the copious extracts which have been given from Rothes' *Relation* and Wariston's *Diary*, it may perhaps be inferred that, when the Covenant was sworn by a congregation with uplifted hands, the members were not asked to subscribe individually ; and, on the other hand, that, when many subscribed, they were not asked to hold up their hands and swear, the mere subscribing of such a solemn oath being regarded as swearing, just as people nowadays are said to " make oath " when they sign an affidavit.[1] The procedure may not have been invariable, but there can be no dubiety as to the mode which was followed at the Canonry of Ross :—

" The Covenant was red out, and the heads therof declaired ; and soe the people went on and subscryvit. Evrie honest man in the toun that could subscryve did soe ; uthers that could not gave power to a nottar to doe it for

[1] In a Latin epistle from the Scottish Churches to the Swiss, appended to William Spang's *Historia Motuum*, 1641, it is said : " Wherefore, being led by serious repentance, they resolved to renew the Covenant with the Confession of Faith, which they first signed in a body with their handwriting ; and afterwards, a solemn fast having been proclaimed, they confirmed these publicly in the churches by an oath, holding up their right hands with much moaning and many tears."

L

them : which being endit, the heads wer againe repeated, and efter ane short exhortatione to constancie, evrie man and woman in the kirk holding up their hands, the oath was solemnlie taken, and the actione concludit with the blessing."

This was on Sabbath the 6th of May ; and the account of it gladdened the hearts of the nobles in Edinburgh on the 9th. That account was transmitted by the Earl of Sutherland, the Master of Berridale, and Lord Reay, who, with the assistance of Lord Lovat and others, had received a joyful assent to the Covenant in Inverness, Forres, Elgin, and Fortrose, not only by the inhabitants of those towns, but by " the greatest part of all sorts benorth Spey." Their account is embodied in Rothes' *Relation* (pp. 104–110, 127). It was on the 25th of April that the gentry of each shire signed at Inverness :—

" It was profest by all, that it was the joyfullest day that ever they saw, or ever was sein in the North ; and it was marked as a speciall mark of God's goodnes towards these parts, that so many different clans and names, among whome was nothing before bot hostilitie and blood, wer mett together in one place for such a good cause, and in so peaceable a manner, as that nothing was to be seen and heard bot mutuall imbracements, with heartie praise to God for so happie a unione." [1]

Next day, one of the bailies ordered the drummer " to touck the drum," and command " all these that feared God to come presentlie to the tolbooth and subscryve the Covenant." The drummer, misunderstanding the order, " added unto it sum penaltie of goods, etc.," which " gave occasione to our adversaries to callumniate our proceidings."

---

[1] Andrew Cant's exhortation on this occasion is included in *A Collection of several Remarkable and Valuable Sermons, Speeches, and Exhortations at Renewing and Subscribing the National Covenant*, etc., printed in 1741, and reprinted in 1799.

On the 7th of July, the Marquis of Hamilton, the King's Commissioner, desired (Rothes' *Relation*, pp. 181, 182) "that people sould not be forced to subscryve the Covenant, that no unlawfull nor hard meanes sould be used to persuade or enforce them to it." To which it was promptly replied, "that none wer forced to subscryve, onlie they wer persuadit by good reasones, and the mater was so holy, that they held it irreligious to use wicked meanes for advanceing so good a work." Before the end of that month, the Aberdeen Doctors informed Henderson, Dickson, and Cant (*Generall Demands*, 1663, p. 6), that they had heard, *inter alia*, that, on account of the Covenant, some pastors and prelates had been forced to flee to foreign countries for fear of their lives; and that those, who stayed at home, durst scarcely appear on the highways or streets. To which Henderson and Dickson replied (pp. 42, 44) that they knew of no pastors who had been forced to flee to foreign countries, but had heard of some who had gone to Court of their own accord, to escape from their creditors, and to make lies between the King and his people; and some they knew who wilfully refused to stay with their flocks and deserted them, because they had subscribed. As for the prelates, they had not been asked to subscribe the Covenant; and their flight seemed "rather to have proceeded from inward furies of accusing conscience," or from fear of a storm, which, being raised by their own doings, they could easily prognosticate. Further :—

"We answere that we have seen in this land the day of the Lord's power, wherein his people have most willingly offered themselves in multitudes, like the dew of the morning : that others of no small note have offered their subscriptions, and have been refused till tyme should try that they joine in sincerity, from love to the cause and not from the feare of men : and that no threatnings have been used, except of the deserved judgement of God ; nor force, except the force of reason, from the high respects which we owe to religion, to our King, to our native countrey, to ourselves, and to the posterity; which hath been to some a greater constraint than any externall violence; and we wish may prevaile also with you."

Noble words! It is a thousand pities that the Covenanters did not abide by them. In August 1639, the General Assembly petitioned the High Commissioner and the Privy Council to enjoin the subscribing of the Covenant " by all his Majestie's subjects, of what rank and quality soever." The petition was granted on the 30th of that month, and the Assembly thereupon (*Acts of the General Assembly*, Church Law Society edition, pp. 40, 42) ordained, under all ecclesiastical censure,

" That all the masters of universities, colledges, and schooles, all schollers at the passing of their degrees, all persons suspect of Papistry or any other errour, and, finally, all the members of this Kirk and Kingdome, subscribe the same with these words prefixed to their subscription :— ' *The article of this Covenant, which was at the first subscription referred to the determination of the Generall Assembly, being determined, and thereby the Five Articles of Perth, the government of the Kirk by bishops, the civill places and power of kirkmen, upon the reasons and grounds contained in the Acts of the Generall Assembly, declared to be unlawfull within this Kirk, we subscribe according to the determination foresaid.*' "

On the 6th of June 1640, Parliament (*Acts of Parliament*, v. 270) ratified this Act of Assembly, and ordained the Covenant " to be subscryveit by all his Majestie's subjectis of what ranke and quality soevir under all civill paines." And on the 5th of the following August, the Assembly (*Acts of the General Assembly*, p. 45) ordained :—

" That if any expectant [*i.e.* probationer] shall refuse to subscribe the Covenant, he shall be declared uncapable of a pedagogie, teaching of a school, reading at a kirk, preaching within a presbyterie, and shall not have libertie of residing within a burgh, universitie, or colledge ; and if they continue obstinate to be processed."

By far the most interesting of the original copies (or, as Wariston would have called them, principal copies) of the National Covenant still known to exist, is the one in Edinburgh Municipal Museum. The extreme measurements are : across the top, 3 feet 10⅞ inches, and from top to bottom 3 feet 7⅝ inches. On the front there are about thirteen hundred and fifty signatures and initials, all autograph. Among them are many of the leading nobles, including Montrose, Rothes, Cassillis, and Loudoun ; and such prominent ministers as Harry Rollock, Edinburgh ; David Dickson, Irvine ; and Alexander Henderson, Leuchars. Johnston of Wariston's signature is also there. So, too, is that of " M. Patrik Henrysone, publict lector "— the reader of St. Giles, who officiated immediately before Dean Hanna on the fateful 23rd of July 1637. One of the most carefully written signatures is that of Sir Andrew Moray of Balvaird, the minister of Abdie. Johne Cunynghame appends to his name, " till daith." E. Johnestoun adds to his, " with my ♡." In a small neat hand, one has written : " Exurgat Deus et dissipentur omnes inimici eius Johannes Paulicius manu propria." The back is also crowded with names, about nineteen hundred of which are autograph signatures, and about nine hundred have been written by notaries. In all, therefore, there are about four thousand one hundred and fifty names on this skin. The nine hundred illiterates comprise craftsmen of various kinds, and many—simply designated " workman "—who were probably unskilled labourers.

It has long been supposed that this was the copy which was first signed in the Greyfriars' Church, and, as was believed, in the churchyard.   One would fain trow that it was the actual copy which was read by Wariston in the church on the 28th of February 1638, and which the nobles and barons signed that evening.   So far as size is concerned it might well be that copy.   But there is one distinguishing feature in it which is hard to reconcile with that idea.   The text of the Covenant is followed by the sentence (beginning, *The article of this Covenant*) which, the General Assembly, on the 30th of August 1639, ordered to be prefixed to the subscriptions.   The ink with which this sentence has been written is the same in colour as the lines which immediately precede it, and the handwriting is also the same.   That sentence could not possibly have been there before the famous Glasgow Assembly met at the end of 1638 ; [1] and it is difficult to believe that it was added after the signatures had been adhibited.

On the back of the document, however, are the words : " At the South Kirk of Edinburgh the threttein, twentie, and xxvii dayis of Marche, 1638."   It is possible that the notary, who wrote this and the names which follow it, may have written the wrong year by mistake, but that does not seem likely.   The question remains, Which church was then known as the South Kirk of Edinburgh ?   A communion cup of Old Greyfriars, bearing the date 1633, is inscribed : " For the chvrch of the svth vest parich of Edinbvrghe " (Burns' *Old Scottish Communion Plate*, pp. 222, 223).   The

---

[1] On the 20th of December 1638 the General Assembly approved the National Covenant " in all the heads and articles thereof," and ordained " that all ministers, masters of universities, colledges, and schooles, and all others who have not already subscribed the said Confession and Covenant, shall subscribe the same with these words prefixed to the subscription, viz., *The article of this Covenant, which was at the first subscription referred to the determination of the Generall Assembly, being now determined at Glasgow, in December 1638, and thereby the Five Articles of Perth, and the governement of the Kirk by bishops, being declared to be abjured and removed, the civill places and power of kirkmen declared to be unlawfull, we subscrive according to the determination of the said free and lawfull Generall Assembly holden at Glasgow* " (*Acts of the General Assembly*, p. 31).

communion cups and laver of the Tron Church, dated 1633, were for " the south east parish " of Edinburgh (*ibid.* pp. 348, 520). The inscription on the Tron cups, but not on the laver, was recut in 1756. In Rothiemay's *Bird's-Eye View of Edinburgh*, 1647, the Greyfriars' Church is called " The West Kirk or Grayfrier Kirk." The West Kirk was the name commonly applied to St. Cuthbert's, or more properly the West Kirk outwith Edinburgh. The Old Kirk—which long met in the central part of St. Giles, including the south transept—is, in its *Session Register*, called "the Old or South Kirk " on the 13th of January 1702. If it could be shown that the Greyfriars' Church was in 1638 sometimes called the South Kirk, it might be argued that the Municipal Museum Covenant was signed in the churchyard, for the words are, " *At* the South Kirk of Edinburgh," not " *in* "; though it is highly improbable that, in the month of March, people would subscribe in the open air when they could do so inside the church.[1] One is loath to discredit or disprove the picturesque tradition ; but truth is more than sentiment ; and one, who has helped to perpetuate the tradition, can only make amends by showing the unsatisfactoriness of the basis on which it rests.

In closing, it may not be amiss to mention that the National Covenant of 1638 (embodying the Covenant, or Confession of Faith, of 1580–81) has often been confounded, even by historians, with the Solemn League and Covenant, which had the same object but a wider scope, and was not drawn up until 1643.

[1] Mr. Moir Bryce has found the following entry in the *Register of Edinburgh Town Council* (xv. 321), 1st November 1643 : "The same day compered James Cochrane, mer^d, and produced the first Covenant, which the Counsell ordaines to be put up in the charter hows." This may have been the copy of the National Covenant now in the Municipal Museum.

IX

THE COVENANTING PERIOD, 1638 TO 1660

The fiery cross for liberty—civil as well as religious—
which, as narrated in the preceding chapter by Dr. Hay
Fleming, received its vital spark in the Church of the Greyfriars, was destined ere long to illuminate the whole country.
Copies of the Covenant, provided by the tearful but in-
defatigable Wariston, were carried from church to church
and place to place in both Edinburgh and Leith ; and there,
under the influence of the magnetic eloquence of Alexander
Henderson, Andrew Ramsay, and Harry Rollock, they
received the signed imprimatur of multitudes of people. On
the 4th of the following month of May [1638] the Town
Council appointed Henderson, the compiler of the Covenant
and leader of the church, to the second charge at Greyfriars
in succession to Mr. Fairlie—" Understanding the literature
and qualificatioun of Maister Alexander Hendersoun, present
Minister of the Kirk of Luchers in Fyif, to supplye the
said plaice, hes elected, out of the lyittes [leets] presentlie
maid, the said Mr. Alexander Hendersoun to the said vacant
plaice of the Ministrie of ye said paroche and stipend appointed thairto." [1] Among other articles of information, says
Dr. M'Crie,[2] sent up to the Scottish bishops then in London,
by their friends in Scotland, was the following : " That the
Council of Edinburgh have made choice of Mr. Alexander
Henderson to be helper to Mr. Andrew Ramsay, and
intend to admit him without advice or consent of
the bishops." The two great leaders in the Covenanting

[1] *Council Records*, xv. 55.   [2] *Life of Alexander Henderson*, p. 17.

View from Churchyard—looking North.

movement, Henderson and Ramsay, were therefore, for the moment, officially conjoined in the ministry of Greyfriars. Eight months later, on 2nd January 1639, the Council elected Henderson to one of the vacant places in the Great Church ; [1] and on 3rd July 1640, Ramsay, Henderson, and three others, " ministeris of this burgh for the present," handed over to the Council certain sums of money bequeathed by Lady Yester and Dr. Arnot.[2]   In the month of November 1638, the famous meeting of the General Assembly—at which the whole Episcopal régime, with its bishops and archbishops, service-books and books of canons, was declared at an end—was held in Glasgow.   Henderson was elected Moderator, and it is to be noted that he is described in the List of Assembly as " minister at Luchers "[3]—not Greyfriars.   Among the bishops who were at this time deprived of their offices was James Fairlie, the ex-minister of Greyfriars, and who, in consequence, suffered severely during the next three or four years from poverty.   His case excited universal regret, as he had given great satisfaction in the performance of his ministerial duties, and " yet no place could be gotten to him to deliver him from that extreamitie of povertie wherwith long he had been vexed." [4]   Ultimately, on the recommendation of the Commissioners of Assembly, he was appointed in 1644 to the parish church at Lasswade.   The clouds of war now began to assemble, and on the 15th of March 1639, a proclamation was issued by the magistrates of Edinburgh summoning all the burghers to attend their colours in the " Greyfriars Kirkyard "—the grass park previously referred to—" in their best apparel and armour, on 26th instant at eight o'clock in the morning." The officer in command was Colonel Robert Munro, to whose care the arms from the city armour-house were sent.[5]

---

[1] *Council Records*, xv. 77.   [2] *Ibid.* xv. 143.
[3] *Records of the Kirk*, Peterkin, i. 110.
[4] Baillie, i. 372.   [5] Dean of Guild's Accounts.

M

On the renewal of open hostilities between King Charles and the Scots, the Castle of Edinburgh, which was held for the King by Patrick Ruthven, an officer of considerable distinction in the wars of Gustavus Adolphus, was closely invested, in May 1640, by a strong force under General Leslie. Four batteries were erected by the Covenanters, one, armed with six guns, being placed " in the north-west end of the Gray Friers." [1] At this date there would be few buildings intervening between the foot of the graveyard, where the battery was erected, and the Grassmarket. Leslie's object was to utilise this battery to " dismount a few gunnes that stood upon the high round of the Castle opposite to that battery "; [2] and it has to be explained that the embrasures which now protect the guns in the Half-Moon Battery were only added in 1683. In the month of July the General Assembly was held at Aberdeen, under the presidency of Mr. Andrew Ramsay as Moderator. The Church of the Greyfriars had by this time come to occupy an important position in the religious life of the city, and the want of a bell to summon the parishioners to worship began to be seriously felt. Accordingly, the kirk-session entered into an arrangement with the Corporation of Hammermen whereby, for an annual payment of forty pounds Scots, the great bell of the Magdalene Chapel in the Cowgate might " be rung to ye preiching of ye Grayfrier Kirk." The agreement was to last during the pleasure of the Hammermen, " and, with all yat, ye deacon should stryve to get Alexr. Meikle for ye ringing theirof." [3] Meikle

---

[1] *Memorie of the Somervills*, ii. 223.   [2] *Ibid.*

[3] " 15 May 1641. The quilk day ye deacon reported that ye Grayfrier Kirk desirit yat ye great bell m⁰ be rung to ye preiching of ye Grayfrier Kirk, and yat they wald give fourtie pundis yearly for ringing thairof. Quilk report being considerit, and they being riply and weill advisit yair with, assent to ye bell-ringing upon condition that they should not be restricted yairto, but during their pleasure, and with all yat, ye deacon should stryve to get Alexr. Meikle for ye ringing theirof as he could." *M.S. Records of the Hammermen of Edinburgh*, vol. iii.; communicated by Mr. John Smith.

belonged to the family of bell founders on the Castlehill that made the bell which was placed in 1691 in the tower of the Greyfriars, as well as the peal of thirty-two bells in St. Giles which our City Fathers so foolishly disposed of by auction about twenty years ago.

On Tuesday, 20th July 1641, the General Assembly met at St. Andrews; but it was agreed that, as Parliament was sitting in Edinburgh at the same time, the Assembly should, at the special request of the Committee of Estates, transfer the place of meeting to Edinburgh. In accordance with this resolution, the Assembly on the 27th did " sit down in the Grey Friar Kirk," [1] where the Earl of Wemyss acted as the royal Commissioner, and Henderson as Moderator. As the latter is again described in the List of Assembly as minister at Leuchars, we may conclude that Henderson did not accept the appointment by the Town Council to Grey-friars. By an Act of 24th December 1641, [2] the city was divided into six separate parishes. Messrs. Rollock and Henderson were appointed ministers to the North Parish; while Ramsay was translated from the Greyfriars to the South Parish. Despite what is stated in the *Fasti*, there can be no question that Ramsay was minister of the first charge in Greyfriars from 1620 down to the year 1641. Besides being highly cultured, he was a man of a superior type of character. Bishop Guthry describes him as " a guid, modest, learned, and godlie man, full of piety and learning," and as an " ornament to the Church of Scotland." [3] He showed his continued interest in the University of Edinburgh, in which he had filled the position of Rector and Professor of Divinity, by bequeathing to it a sum of £423, 6s. 8d. Scots to found four bursaries in Divinity. His eldest son, Sir Andrew Ramsay of Abbotshall, was more than once Lord Provost of Edinburgh, and by his Deed

[1] Spalding's *Troubles*, i. 243.   [2] *Council Records*, xv. 214.
[3] Guthry's *Memoirs*.

of Settlement,[1] dated 21st June 1687, he mortified the sum of 10,000 merks to the University, " for the memory of his dearest father, Mr. Andrew Ramsay, late Minister of Edinburgh and Rector of the College." The sixth and last parish was to be that of the South-West, or Greyfriars, and for it the Council " designe thar boundis lyand upoun the south syd of the hie street from Forresteris Wynd inclusive, doun to the Cowgait, and alongs downe the Cowgait to the fute of the said wynd called Forresteris Wynd exclusive, and that boundis upon the south syde of the Cowgait fra the Potterraw Port downe the west syd of the hors wynd to the west port, including the Colledge heirin. And ordains the parochin to be callit the South-West parochin of this burgh in all tyme coming ; and appoyntis for yr churche the churche in the gray freir yaird ; and appoyntis for yr ministers [sic] Mr. George Gillespie." [2] Each parish was to be " governed in matteris ecclesiasticall be their own severall Ministeris and Session ; And ilk Session to consist of the Provest, Baillies, the Ministeris of the parishe, and four elders and four deakens." The bailie of the South-West Quarter was also ordered to attend the meetings of the Grey-friars' Kirk-Session to be held on the Friday afternoons at two o'clock. The appointment of Mr. Gillespie as successor to Mr. Ramsay gave much satisfaction to the congregation, and his nomination was confirmed by an Act of Council dated 21st September 1642. Although at this time only twenty-nine years of age, he soon proved himself a brilliant preacher and capable debater, and between the years 1643–47 he was sent as one of the Scottish Commissioners to the Westminster Assembly, where he greatly distinguished himself. He presented the Confession of Faith to the General Assembly held in Edinburgh on 4th August 1647. During his prolonged visits to England, he was paid, by order of the Town Council, his usual stipend as minister of Greyfriars.

[1] *Council Records, Ch. Ho. Inv.* v. 2816.   [2] *Council Records,* xv. 214.

Sir Alexander Clerk, the Provost, died in the autumn of the
year 1643, and was buried on 5th September within the
precincts of the church.   Strict orders were issued that the
"haill Counsell sall accompanie his corps to the Grayfreirs,"
the bailies, dean of guild, and treasurer dressed in red
gowns, and "the rest of the Counsell with blak gowns, and
to returne from thence in dooll blacks."[1]   His tombstone
was removed, at the restoration of the church in 1857, to
the outer side of the north wall.   Mr. Mungo Law, who was
translated from Dysart to the second charge at Greyfriars on
27th March 1644,[2] also acted as a minister on the staff of
the army;   and in that capacity, on 2nd February, he
witnessed the inglorious defeat of Argyll's forces by Montrose at the battle of Inverlochy.   In September 1647
Gillespie was transferred to the North Church of St. Giles,[3]
and was elected Moderator of the General Assembly held in
July of the following year, when his intellectual powers
were at their height.   His health gave way, and as the
Cowgate was then considered the most sheltered part of the
city—the *Riviera* of Edinburgh—the Town Council provided for him a house in the High School Yards: "The
Counsell, taking to consideratioun the sadd conditioun of
Mr. George Gillespie, one of our ministeris, be reasone of
his heavie sicknes in Kerkadie, and that he is desyreous
to end his dayes att God's pleasor wtin this burt, to qlk
effect most necessyr and convenient is it that a house be
prepaired for him of the best air and wyer [other] commodities.   Thairfoir, ordaines James Rucheid [and others]
to take the best courss they can qrby the houss in the hie
scoole yaird, presentlie occupyed be the relict of wmqle
Doctor Johne Sharp, be provydit to him."[4]   He did not live
to enjoy the gift, as he died at Kirkcaldy on 16th December
1648, at the early age of thirty-five.   "His learning, acute-

[1] *Council Records*, xv. 309.   [2] *Ibid.* xv. 340.
[3] *Ibid.* xvi. 208.   [4] *Ibid.* xvii. 58, 11th October 1648.

ness, and powers of application, illustration, and persuasion," says one writer,[1] "rendered him of vast service in the Assembly of Divines at Westminster, as well as in the Church Courts. Even Lauderdale and other statesmen quailed so much in arguing with him, that the Earl of Glencairn declared 'there is no standing before this great and mighty man.'" On the 22nd March 1648 the Council nominated Mr. William Rait, minister at Brechin, as Gillespie's successor in Greyfriars, and they also appointed a deputation of councillors to present him for acceptance to the Kirk-Session. Their report is recorded at length in the Council Register, and from it we learn that the meeting with the Session, along with "yair Moderator, Mr. Mungo Law, together with a verie considerable number of honest nighbors, memberis of that same parochin," was held on the 28th, and that, after due consideration, "the whole members as one man, with great applause, doeth accept most kyndlie, and Imbrace with all heartie Thanksgiving, the foirsaid presentatioun and nominatioun of that worthie Instrument in the Kirk of God."[2] For some unknown reason, Mr. Rait—the worthy instrument in the Kirk of God —did not accept office, as there is a further notice in the Register that, on 18th August, the North-East Kirk was the only one in the city provided with two ministers. Mr. Robert Trail, minister of Elie, was, therefore, nominated on 7th November, and confirmed on 4th April 1649 to be colleague to Mungo Law.[3] The reception accorded to Mr. Trail on his induction to Greyfriars was of an unusually cordial character. After receiving in the South-East Parish Church the right hand of fellowship from the assembled city ministers and elders, he was entertained to dinner by the Town Council and made a burgess and guild brother of the

---

[1] Rev. Hew Scott, in *Fasti*, i. 21.
[2] *Council Records*, xv. 268.
[3] *Ibid.* xvii. 132.

Rev. ROBERT TRAIL,

Minister of Greyfriars (1649-1660),

city. Probably this is the earliest mention of an induction dinner on record.[1] Unfortunately, considerable contention had arisen within the whole body of the Church owing to the fierce desire to abolish everything that tended towards formality in divine service, and thereby savoured of Popery or Prelacy. Knox's liturgy had been replaced in 1645 by the Directory, which was an attempt to bring about uniformity of worship based on Presbyterian principles, on both sides of the Tweed; and, as usual in every phase of human life, the extremists became, for the time, the victors. The novations, or innovations, in religion had now assumed a different signification from those of the pre-Covenanting times. They may be said to have commenced in 1640, when learning began to be discountenanced. Knox's liturgy permitted the use of read as well as of "conceived" or *extempore* prayers; but all set or printed forms of prayer were now given up as unspiritual, and *extempore* prayer became the rule. Even the Lord's Prayer grew out of fashion, as too formal, and a "threadbare prayer." The Psalter down to 1638 consisted of the 150 Psalms, with Hymns and Doxologies, or "Conclusions," rendered so as to suit the great variety of metres into which the Psalms were translated. The use of the Doxologies now ceased, and the new party also objected to the minister kneeling for private devotion when he entered the pulpit. The flowers provided by the Town Council during the summer thenceforth disappeared from the communion tables, and the churches themselves became as

[1] *Council Records*, xvii. 125. " 21 March 1649. Mr. Ro⸱ Trael and Mr. Georg Hutchisone, twa of the new electit Ministers of this burgh," to be received by the ministers and elders in the South-East Parish Church on Friday next in the morning, "and ordaines a dinner to be given to the saids Ministers, and the Thesaurer to pay the expenses yrof; and ordaines the dean of gild and his counsell to admitt and resave the saids Ministers Ro⸱ Traill and George Hutchisone to be burgesses and gild broyr of this brugh for pay⸱ of the ordinar dewtie, and ordaines the dean of gild to delyver the samen back againe to them, and to dispenss w⸱ yr armes and wyer [other] small dewes dew to be payit be ym at yr admissioun."

other buildings in the eyes of the community. Down to
1645, Henderson and the other leaders of the Church
strongly opposed all these novations, but without
effect, owing to the increasing influence of the English
sectaries. At the Assembly held in Edinburgh in
July 1649, " ther wer werey many ministeris depossed,"
says Balfour, " for maintaining the last expeditione into
England," and among these was Ramsay, the ex-minister
of Greyfriars. " Bot the current of the tymes went so, that
in respecte they wald not dance to the play of the leaders,
Douglas, Dickson, Cant, Guthrie, and *Law* "—of the Greyfriars—" they wer deposed from the ministeriall office." [1]
And yet, as Balfour observes, Ramsay had spent fifty-three
years of his life as a minister. Minute shades of differences
in religious and, particularly, in political opinion began to
to be discovered, and the religious leaders, the ministers,
became, like the Roman clergy of old, infected with the
lust of power. A late writer has declared, truly enough,
that the " assumption of political power by the Church was,
doubtless, the actual cause of all their contentions." [2]
Purging the roll, as it was termed, became the favourite
occupation, and internal dissension began to rend the
grand old Church, to the upbuilding of which John Knox and
his fellow-reformers had devoted their lives. The news of
the approach of Cromwell and his legionaries in the early
part of the summer of 1650 brought about the usual call to
arms ; and the Magistrates of Edinburgh issued an order
for all " fensible " persons in the city to meet on the 10th of
May, in the Greyfriars' Yard—the grass park already referred
to. Five days later a day of thanksgiving was held in all
the churches of the city to commemorate the defeat and
capture of the gallant Montrose.; and on that occasion
the " new Psalme buikis wer red and ordanit to be sung

[1] *Annals*, Balfour, iii. 419.
[2] Dr. David Laing, in preface to Baillie's *Letters*, vol. i. lxix.

throw all the kingdome."[1]   The author of the new version of the Psalms was Francis Rous, a younger son of Sir Anthony Rous, and a native of Cornwall. He was several times returned as member of the English House of Commons, and was also chosen as a lay Commissioner to the Westminster Assembly of Divines. Latterly he became Provost of Eton. The acceptance of this version by the General Assembly was intended as another step towards uniformity of worship on both sides of the border; and, although unsuccessful as regards England, this English book of Psalms has continued to maintain its position as the authorised version in Scotland down to the present day. In the older version of the Psalms—that allied to Knox's liturgy down to 1638—it is worthy of note that, in the printed editions, the Psalms are almost invariably accompanied with the tunes set to music; while, in the edition of 1635, the tunes are harmonised in the usual four parts. This implies that, prior to the year 1650, there must have existed a much greater knowledge of sacred music than was, subsequent to that date, to be found in this country until within recent years; but in those days instruction in singing occupied an ordinary place in education, and music schools were also well supported by the then City Fathers.[2] In Germany —the home of the Reformation—the subtle and refining influences of both music and poetry found expression in the beautiful Lutheran Hymns.

Towards the end of July, Cromwell with his army of sectaries made his appearance at Restalrig and Meadowbank; but Leslie, in anticipation, had erected a long line of formidable entrenchments extending from the west end of Leith Links to the Calton Hill and Abbeyhill. Foiled in his attack on Leith, Cromwell ultimately swung round

[1] Nicoll's *Diary*, 11.

[2] Cf. Dr. David Laing's interesting account of the two versions of our Psalm Books and his remarks on singing, in Baillie's *Letters*, iii. pp. 525 to 560.

N

Arthur's Seat and Craigmillar, and encamped on the Braid
and Blackford Hills. During the whole of the month of
August the contending armies spent the time in attempting
to out-manœuvre each other ; while our Scottish ministers
occupied themselves in the congenial business of purging
the roll of their army. Even the night before the fatal
battle of Dunbar, " our Scottis leaders wer in purging the
Scottis airmy, as gif thair haid bene no danger," [1]
says Nicoll, the contemporary diarist ; and he further
assures us that " divisiounes, haitrent, and malice
still increst throw the kingdome." [2] It was an unhappy
period in the history of our Church ; and it is to
be remembered that it was the controversial spirit en-
gendered by the extravagant claims of the ministry at
this time that has been the continued cause of the numerous
defections from our national Zion. Cromwell entered
Edinburgh on the 7th of September, and the 24th October
was ordered to be held as a day of thanksgiving for the
victory at Dunbar—a request which the Edinburgh ministers
refused to implement. All the churches and other large
buildings on the eastern and southern sides of the city
were handed over for the accommodation of the Cromwellian troops, and among those so selected was the church
of the Greyfriars. As the church was turned into a barrack-
room, the wild soldiery had no hesitation in smashing and
utilising the pews and other woodwork of the building for
firewood, while the broken windows provided ample
ventilation. All the other churches suffered in a similar
manner, and Nicoll tells us that they " wer all wasted, thair
pulpits, dasks, loftes, saittes, windows, dures, locks, bandis,
and all uther thair decormentis, wer all dung doun to the
ground by these Inglische sodgeris, and burnt to ashes." [3]
The church remained in the occupation of the troopers
down to the year 1653, and it is certainly remarkable that

---

[1] Nicoll's *Diary*, 28.   [2] *Ibid.* 30.   [3] *Ibid.* 35.

Communion Plate of Old Greyfriars' Church.

the beautiful communion cups, four in number, as well as the baptismal laver and basin, should have escaped their clutches.   Two of the cups were presented to the church in 1633, and the other two in 1644.   The silver laver and basin seem to have been made in the year 1649, and the latter is engraved on the back, "1649 Basen and Laer Wyes [weighs] 74 uncis 4 dropis."   Under the foot of the laver there is this inscription, "Reneued anno domini 1707.   William Neilson, Dean of Gild," and it is, therefore, evident that both the cups and the baptismal service were gifted to the church by the city.   Mr. Mungo Law, the senior minister of Greyfriars, was one of the extremists, and, therefore, more occupied with the cares of politics than in ministering to the spiritual needs of his congregation.   While attending a meeting of the Committee of Estates in 1651, at Alyth, he had the misfortune to be captured by the Ironsides and carried off to England, where he remained until January 1653.[1]   In the early part of this year the church was once more handed over to the congregation; and on 18th May the Town Council appointed a deputation of bailies, the dean of guild, and others to confer with the minister and kirk-session regarding the dilapidated condition of the building. To raise the necessary funds the Council gave instructions, two days later, that a voluntary collection should be made at the doors of all the churches in the city, and on the 15th of June overseers were appointed to carry out the necessary repairs.[2]   A few months afterwards, Sir James M'Gill of Cranston M'Gill and Sir John Gilmour were permitted to erect family pews at their own expense, and to make use of them for four years without payment of rent.[3]   It appears from a petition by Mungo Law and his kirk-session, read at a meeting of Council on 22nd June 1655, that the repairs at the church had been carried through mainly at

[1] *Fasti*, i. 45.
[2] *Council Records*, xviii. 26, 30.   [3] *Ibid*. xviii. 72, 9th November 1653.

the expense of the parishioners; but, their funds being now exhausted, they sought a contribution from the Council towards the erection of a loft.[1] The Council granted the kirk-session the sum of £400 Scots, and also gave them permission to use other two lofts free of rent for four years.[2] At Whitsunday 1654, five out of the ten city ministers were in arrear of their stipends to the extent, collectively, of a sum of £8160 Scots; while down to March in the following year, the stipends still remained unpaid.[3] Three years later, to save the ministers from actual starvation, some of the individual members of the Council generously subscribed and advanced the money out of their own pockets![4] With the object of increasing the number of the city parishes to ten, the Greyfriars' Church was divided into two in 1656 by the erection of a solid wall of masonry. The easter half was handed over to Mr. Mungo Law, and the wester portion to Mr. Robert Trail, while one kirk-session, consisting of eight elders and eight deacons, was appointed to act for both churches.[5] The alterations, including the insertion of a door on the north side of the Easter Church, were evidently completed by the summer of the following year, when two hundred tickets or tokens were issued to Mr. Mungo Law.[6] On Sunday, the 23rd January 1659, a violent storm threatened to unroof the Wester Church, and Mr. Robert Trail and the whole of his congregation were forced to seek safety in flight.[7] The Dean of Guild's Accounts show that the sum of £66, 13s. 4d. Scots was paid for repairs to the roof, and £50 Scots for other " repairation."

The extent and variety of powers exercised by the kirk-session of the Greyfriars can, perhaps, be more readily understood from a perusal of some extracts from the record

[1] *Council Records*, xviii. 184.   [2] *Ibid*. xviii. 238.
[3] *Ibid*. xviii. 160, 166.   [4] *Ibid*. xix. 281.
[5] *Ibid*. xix. 179, 188.   [6] Dean of Guild's Accounts.
[7] Nicoll's *Diary*, 225—" to flie out of the church for feir of their lyves. This tempest of wind continued mony dayis thaireftir."

of the General Sessions—including that of Greyfriars—of Edinburgh, during the Cromwellian period :—

2nd Feb. 1657.—Item, findis it conduceable for the behove of the poore, that everie Session shall take up a roll of honest and creditable men to collect at the kirk doors, both Sabbath and week dayes.

It is againe earnestlie desired and seriouslie recomended to each elder and deacon in their owne bounds, to go throw and take exact tryell that none be found vaging or standing at closse heads, profaning the Lord's Day.

1st June 1657.—To advance to the deacons distributors, who gives the bursars in the colledge, and poore schoolers in the gramer schoole, their pensions and month's pensions beforehand.

6th June 1657.—To confer with [Town] Councell anent the qwaikers, whose blasphemous tenents and cariage is . . . likely to bring a judgement if it be not restrained.

Item, to speak to the Councell anent the Grayfreir Kirkyard, which is shamefully abused.

To visit the prisoners in the Abbay . . . being, as they professe, readie to sterve.

7th Sept. 1657.—It is thought fitt that no poore prentise shall be bound to any man but such as the deacon shall declare [before the Session] to be ane honest man.

5th April 1658.—The Magistrats is to tak course with those who go vaging upon the streets and on the Castellhill, Grayfreir Yaird, Colledge Church Yaird, and other pairts. The Magistrats is to cause sum Inglis souldiours goe along the streets and those outparts above written, both before sermon and after sermon, and lay hold upon both young and old whom they find out of yir houses or out of ye church.

X

THE RESTORATION PERIOD, 1660 TO 1688

The resignation, or, in reality, the deposition of Richard Cromwell, son and successor of " the late usurper," and the assumption of political power in England by the military, forced General Monk, the commander of the English forces in Scotland, into the position of dictator.   Emboldened by Scottish opinion, and especially that of Robert Douglas, the leader of the Church, and of many of the ministers,[1] he summoned a meeting of his officers in October 1659 in the historic Church of the Greyfriars,[2] and there they " did retene their principles, that is, not to be commanded by a sword governament, bot by a parliament lauchfullie and legalie constitute, for obtening, quhairof, thai haid bene sworne."[3]   At the head of an army of 6000 men he crossed the Tweed at Berwick on 1st January 1660, and began his triumphal march to London—the *iter borealis*—which eventuated in the course of five months in the restoration of monarchy in the person of the apparently careless but clever King Charles II.   The return of the Stuart King, however, brought in its train a new and disastrous era for Presbyterianism in this country.

Mungo Law, the minister of the East Greyfriars, died in the early part of the month of February 1660, and, on the 24th, the Town Council appointed a committee to discuss with the city ministers as to the settlement of his successor.   At this period the funds at the disposal of the Council were at a low ebb, and payment of Law's stipend

[1] Blair, 340.   [2] *The Covenanters*, Dr. King Hewison, ii. 56.
[3] Nicoll, 258.

had, like that of all the other ministers, fallen considerably
into arrear. Instead of money, a written bond[1] for the
amount due as at the preceding Whitsunday was, therefore,
handed over to Law's children, and in September the
Council managed to pay, "out of the love, favour, and affection they cary to his children," the sum of 625 merks, "as
a quarter's stipend from Whitsunday last bypast to Lambes
last bypast."[2] Despite his intermittent attention to his
parochial duties, Law had managed to retain to the last a
considerable share of personal popularity. His colleague,
Mr. Trail, fared badly at the hands of the new administration, which was anxious, at this date, to publish to the
world the re-establishment of Episcopacy with all its old
arbitrary ways. A meeting of the Committee of Estates
was held in Edinburgh on 23rd August 1660, for the purpose
of framing a provisional government to act until the
assembling of Parliament; and on the same day the Pro-
testers, as they were termed, on a requisition of five ministers,
among whom were James Guthrie and Robert Trail, met in
the house of a burgess named Robert Simpson. Refusing
when summoned to disperse, both Guthrie and Trail, along
with ten others, were arrested, and warded in Edinburgh
Castle, "upon information given to said Committee of a conventicle and private meeting of some remonstrate and protest-
ing ministers."[3] Here Trail lay for ten months, when, having
fallen sick, he was temporarily permitted to return to his
own home. His stipend was sequestrated by the Committee
of Estates; but it was ordered by Act of Parliament to be
paid to him down to Candlemas 1661.[4] On 11th December
1662, he appeared before the Lords of the Privy Council,
and, having refused to sign the oath of allegiance, was
sentenced to be banished furth of the kingdom.[5] To avoid

---

[1] Dated 23rd March 1660. *Council Records*, xx. 125.   [2] *Ibid.* xx. 179.
[3] *Register of Privy Council*, 2nd Series, viii. 465.   [4] Thomson's *Acts*, vii. 57.
[5] *Register of the Privy Council*, 3rd Series, v. i. 303.

imprisonment, he gave his personal obligation to comply with the terms of his sentence :—

"I, Mr. Robert Traill, late Minister at Edinburgh, binds and obliges me to remove myself furth of the King's dominions within a moneth after the date hereof, and not to remain within the same hereafter under the paine of death. In witnes quherof I have subscryved these presents at Edinburgh the eleventh of December 1662."[1]

Owing to the tempestuous weather, Trail experienced difficulty in finding a ship in which to sail to Holland, and on the 23rd the Privy Council granted him a month's further grace in which to take his departure. In his petition, he states that he " is towards the age of sixty years, if not more, and so cannot weill take such a jorney in such a season without evident hazard of his lyfe."[2]

The old claims by James VI. and Charles I. for supremacy in both State and Church were practically revived by the Parliament that sat in Holyrood during the first half of the year 1661. Once more the Privy Council, as the supposed mouthpiece of the King, usurped all the governmental functions and powers of Parliament; and, as the right of appointment of its members was declared by chapter six of that Act to be included within the royal prerogative, the Council became omnipotent and self-contained. In this way, a minority section of the community was enabled, for a period of twenty-eight years, to secure the reins of government in the interests of its Episcopalian co-religionists. The Marquis of Argyll and the pious James Guthrie were the first victims of the new régime, and the latter was the first of a long line of martyrs for the Presbyterian cause, whose ashes found a last resting-place in the old historic graveyard of the Greyfriars. Finally, the Scottish Parliament, on the 27th May 1662, passed the " Act for the

---

[1] *Register of the Privy Council*, 3rd Series, v. i. 303.   [2] *Ibid.* i. 312.

Tombs of ALEXANDER HENDERSON and
Principal CARSTARES.

restitution and re-establishment of the antient government of the church by archbishops and bishops." Thereupon James Sharp, as Archbishop of the Metropolitan See of St. Andrews emerged into the light of day as the director or manager of His Majesty's Scottish Privy Council, and as the destroyer of his old Covenanting friends and brethren, upon whose necks the traitor had raised himself into power. The change in the official religion was celebrated by two contemptible but characteristic acts of meanness. The inscription on the tombstone erected over the grave in the Greyfriars' Churchyard of the distinguished Alexander Henderson was wantonly obliterated by a platoon of soldiers ; while that at Kirkcaldy of George Gillespie, the old minister of Greyfriars, was also mutilated.

Although, as we have seen, Episcopacy had been re-established in this country, it is an extraordinary fact that, down to the Revolution of 1688, no attempt was made to reintroduce Laud's liturgy, or any other form of liturgy practised in England ; while the doctrine and mode of worship contained in Knox's liturgy also remained undisturbed. The only visible change lay in the introduction of bishops and archbishops—all else was Presbyterian. Sir George Mackenzie, the Lord Advocate—better known to history as " Bloody Mackenzie "—wrote, in 1691, a " Vindication of the Government in Scotland during the reign of King Charles II.," which was intended as an *apologia* for his own ruthless conduct. On page 9, he describes, authoritatively, the practice of Church government during that period. He says :—

"The Reader will be astonished, when we inform him ; that the way of Worship in our Church, differed nothing from what the Presbyterians themselves practised (except only, that we used the *Doxologie, the Lord's Prayer,* and in *Baptism, the Creed,* all which they rejected). We had no *Ceremonies, Surplice, Altars, Cross in Baptisms,* nor the meanest of those things which would be allowed

o

in *England* by the *Dissenters*, in way of Accommodation : That the most Able and Pious of their Ministers did hear the Episcopal Clergy Preach, many of them Communicated in the Churches, and almost all the People Communicated also ; so that it cannot be said *that they were Persecuted*, and forced to joyn with an *Unsound*, much less *Heretical* Church, as the *French* Protestants are."

Although an annuity tax of six per cent. on all rentals in the city had been imposed under the statute of 1661,[1] the re-establishment of Episcopacy had greatly increased the difficulty of the Town Council in scraping together sufficient money wherewith to pay the stipends of the ministers, and an Act of Council passed on 4th October 1661 sufficiently explains the situation : " To think of some gift to be asked of His Majesty for maintenance of the clergy in lieu of the former gift of the Bishopric of Orkney, and Deanery of Edinburgh, which are to return to the respective benefited persons by the restitution of Episcopacy."[2] The petition of the Council met with a favourable reception, and in lieu of the Bishoprics of Orkney and Edinburgh, which they had been forced to resign, the Magistrates received the *gift* of the statutory right to levy a tax on wines and strong liquors[3] for the support of the ministers ! But the city treasury was in a sadly depleted condition, and, in order to pay the stipends for the current year, the Council executed a bond for the amount—24,000 merks—and, in security thereof, assigned the royal *gift* of the tax on liquors.[4] It appears that the money was in reality advanced on the personal security of certain of the Town Councillors.[5] The next step was the allocation of a church or cathedral for the use of the new Bishop of Edinburgh ; and, accordingly, on 2nd June 1662, the " East Kirk of Sanct Geills, being the cheafe Kirk of this burgh," was declared by the

---

[1] Thomson's *Acts*, 1661, vii. 244.
[2] *Council Records*, xxi. 28.   [3] *Ibid*. 1662, vii. 398.
[4] *Ibid*. xxii. 14, 19th December 1662.   [5] *Ibid*. xxii. 37.

Town Council " the most propper for that effect." The minister, Mr. Robert Douglas, was, thereupon, transferred to the East Greyfriars' Church, " quhairof Mr. Mungo Law wes last minister, [and] hes been hitherto served be a helper sen his deceis." [1] Mr. Douglas practically succeeded Henderson in the leadership of the Church. He presented the Solemn League and Covenant to Parliament on 12th January 1649, when it was subscribed by all the members, and on five different occasions he was elected Moderator of the General Assembly. On 1st January 1651 he had the honour of crowning Charles II. at Scone, and was among the unfortunates who were seized at Alyth in 1653, and transported to London. He preached at the opening of Heriot's Hospital on 21st June 1659, and, after the Restoration, at the opening of the first Parliament on 1st January 1661.[2] In his correspondence on behalf of the Church, however, he was completely outwitted by the wily Sharp. Along with two other ministers, Douglas received permission to preach, provided he should appear in presence of the Bishop of Edinburgh, and satisfy him before the second of the ensuing month of October. This he failed to do, and was, therefore, put to silence and ordered to leave the city. By the 6th of October five out of the six ministers of Edinburgh were forcibly removed from their churches by the Privy Council. Only one, Lawrie, adhered to the new faith, and, in return for his complaisance, he was promoted to be Dean of St. Giles. Thenceforth he became known as the " Nest-egg." There is no mention of any successor to Mr. Trail in West Greyfriars ; but, in the following month of November, orders were issued by the Council for the demolition of the division wall of the church, and that the stones should be handed over to the Treasurer of Heriot's Hospital to be utilised in the erection of a new south boundary wall to the

---

[1] *Council Records*, xxi. 128.
[2] Cf. Hew Scott's account in the *Fasti*, i. 21–22.

old graveyard in place of the old Flodden Wall, which had
fallen down. The interest of the Hospital in this wall is
not quite apparent. To John Scott, the carpenter who
repaired the pews, the Council handed over the spare pulpit,
along with the sum of 200 merks, as extra payment on account
of the then high price of timber.[1] The Council also appointed, " in the Interim, that either the Common Hall or
the Lady Yester's Kirk be your Paroche Kirk qll the Grayfreir Kirk be repaired." [2] The re-conversion of the Church
into one building formed part of a scheme to reduce the
number of the city parishes to six, according to the previous
arrangement of 1641, and, during the alterations in the
church, the Greyfriars' congregation made use of the newly
erected Parliament Hall.[3] The wall was taken down, and
the two churches thrown into one, in January 1663.[4] Five
ministers who professed to conform to the new régime were
then appointed to the vacant charges in Edinburgh; but,
as the respective kirk-sessions refused to move in the
matter, the Council agreed on the 26th that, as " the easiest
and safest way without emulation," the five ministers whom
they had elected " sall *draw lotts*, and what paroche kirk
they fall to, that they serve yrin during the Counsell's
plesure." [5] The meeting for the drawing took place in
presence of the five applicants on the 29th, when Greyfriars
fell to Mr. John Robertson, minister at Dysart. The Town
Council also succeeded in appointing ministers willing to
conform to the six under or second charges ; but, among
all these appointments, there was not one man to be found
of any distinction. On 6th February the Council agreed to
pay the six principal ministers 2500 merks in name of stipend
and house mail, " and anything els they can seik, yeirlie " ;
and to the six second ministers a sum of £1000 Scots yearly
as their stipend and house mail, " and what els thei can

---

[1] *Council Records*, xxii. 48.   [2] *Ibid.* xxi. 176.   [3] *Ibid.* xxii. 8.
[4] Nicoll, 170, 389.   [5] *Council Records*, xxii. 20.

crave "! [1] In the succeeding month of May, the Council
acknowledged their inability to pay off the arrears of stipend
due to no less than ten ministers or their representatives,
and gave instructions for the issue of bonds or acknowledg-
ments for the respective amounts. Three ministers of the
Greyfriars appear in the list—Robert Douglas, for the sum
of £566, 13s. 4d. ; Robert Trail, for £1691, 15s. 6d. ; and the
executors of Mungo Law, for £936, 6s. 10d. Scots. [2] The
office of the ministry in Edinburgh in those days was apparently the reverse of lucrative. Two months later, the wife
of Mr. Trail appealed to the Council for an advance, as she
found it " necessitate to goe beyond sea to waite upon her
husband "—then an exile—and the humane Council actually
paid her £770 Scots, along with an Act or acknowledgment
for the remainder of their debt—£1000 Scots. [3] At a later
period, in June 1665, she suffered imprisonment for corre-
sponding with her banished husband ; [4] and in 1672, a friend,
Andrew Kennedy, *alias* Weir of Closeburn, was put to the
horn for committing a similar " crime." [5] The minister of
the second charge in Greyfriars was John Stirling, from the
parish of Fulden, who was not elected by the Council until the
25th May 1664 ; [6] and, on 14th July, the Magistrates honoured
the whole of the city ministers by creating them burgesses
and guild brethren of the city. [7] In the early years of the
seventeenth century, the wine in ordinary use at the Communion was claret ; but for that held on the first two
Sundays in April 1666, the Council purchased for distribution among all the city churches " 3 peice of graves wine "
for a sum of £30 sterling. [8] Graves in those days was produced as a red as well as a white wine, although nowadays
it is only treated as a white wine.

Hitherto the upkeep of the roof of the Greyfriars had

---

[1] *Council Records*, xx. 212.   [2] *Ibid*. xxii. 40.   [3] *Ibid*. xxii. 53.
[4] *Fasti*, i. 41.   [5] *Justiciary Records*, ii. 109 ; Scott. H.S.
[6] *Council Records*.   [7] *Ibid*. xxiii. 91.   [8] Dean of Guild's Accounts.

proved a matter of difficulty and expense, and in the annual contracts for the upkeep of the slate-work of all the city churches, that of Greyfriars is invariably excepted and charged for separately. Thus, while the cost, during the years 1666–67 and 1667–68, of repairing the roof of the Greyfriars is entered as £131, 4s. 8d. and £150 respectively, that of all the remaining churches only amounts to a sum of £98 annually. In January 1669, the " tua toofalls in ye Gray freir Kirk " were re-slated, while the roof itself was covered with lead—a costly work, which took three years to complete. Stirling, the minister of the second charge, must have demitted his office in 1669,[1] as we find that, on 8th May of that year, the Council appointed a successor in the person of Alexander Ramsay, minister of Auchinleck. He was transferred to the Old Church three years later, but returned to Greyfriars in 1674. The stipends of the ministers of the second charge, prior to this date, only amounted to the sum of 1500 merks ; but in October 1673, the Council increased their stipends to the sum of 2000 merks.[2] In the following month of November, the Bishop and all the twelve ministers of Edinburgh were admitted burgesses of the city—" Item, the Bishop of Edinburgh and whole ministers admitted Burgesses and Gild brether in the best form, all dews gratis." [3] During the following year, a movement for the holding of a National Synod— in other words, a General Assembly—excited considerable attention within the ranks of the clergy, and the demand was strenuously supported by Robertson, the minister of the Greyfriars. The Bishop of Edinburgh, his diocesan superior, disapproved of the movement, and at his own hand suspended three of the " greatest sticklers for convocation," including Robertson. This sentence was upheld, on appeal to the Privy Council. The imperious Sharp viewed the action of the ministers as showing a contempt for authority, and

[1] 1699 in *Fasti, per incuriam.*　　　[2] Dean of Guild's Accounts.　　　[3] *Ibid.*

greatly desired their punishment by the civil powers.[1] In terms of an order from London, Robertson was "relegated to Auchterless, a private place in the north, to abide there, and not to preach elsewhere."[2]   He submitted in 1675, and pleaded to be restored to his charge, whereupon he was permitted by the Privy Council on 27th April of that year to resume his parochial duties at the Greyfriars. In the month of December, the Town Council took steps to prevent what they considered an infringement of their rights to restrict the burial of burghers to the graveyard of the Greyfriars. From the record we learn that some of the Quakers—a sect then much detested—had purchased a piece of ground in the Pleasance with the view of converting it into a graveyard for their own people. This the Council characterised as an evil example, and they strictly forbade them "to burrie in any place within the toun or liberties yrof but in ye ordinary burriall place."[3]   In those days the city bellmen and their vested interests constituted a power to be reckoned with by the ordinary citizen. It appears that by the year 1676 their services in the matter of burials in the graveyard had threatened to fall into desuetude; and on a complaint by them the Town Council issued a drastic proclamation to the burghers :—

"22 March 1676. All persones that buries yr freinds or oyr relationes without imployeing the belmen to goe for yr saids relationes, shall pay thrie dollairs at least to the Kirk thesaurer for ye use of the poore. The Counsall discharges the grave makers to break ground till testificat be given to them be the Kirk thesaurer yt ye poore are satisfied; and lastly that these persones that hes there chyldring caried upon staves for whom the bellmen is not imployed shall pey four pound scots to the Kirk thesaurer."[4]

Some irregularities in the conduct of public worship must have also occurred, because, on 5th June of this year,

[1] Blair's *Life*, 546.   [2] *Ibid.* 549.
[3] *Council Records*, xxviii. 125.   [4] *Ibid.* xxviii. 148.

instructions were issued by the Town Council—not the
Bishop—that the first and principal minister in each parish
"sall preach ilk Saboth day the foirnoone," and that the
minister of the second charge should conduct the services
in the afternoon, according to the ancient custom practised
by the present ministers since the " restitution of bishops." [1]
Two years later, the unfortunate Robert Trail, who had
been allowed to return to his native land, died in Edinburgh
at the age of seventy-two. During the following winter
Edinburgh became a place of shelter for the wives and
families of most of the " outed, fugitive, and vagrant
preachers and intercommuned persons" throughout the
kingdom. Pinched by poverty, these unfortunate creatures
must have led a miserable existence ; but the ever-watchful
Archbishop Sharp regarded their presence as a source of
danger to the State. Accordingly, the Magistrates, on
14th March 1679, issued a peremptory order for their
removal from the city and its suburbs, within the space
of seven days, under a penalty of £100 sterling, " for each
familie, and imprisonment of yr persons." [2]

The summer of the year 1679 was ushered in by the
murder on 3rd May of the detested Archbishop Sharp on
Magus Moor, near St. Andrews, and was followed by the
rising of the oppressed Covenanters in the western shires
of the country. On the 22nd of June the Duke of Monmouth
obtained an easy victory at Bothwell Bridge, where the
dreadful state of dissension among the Covenanters became
once more the direct cause of their ruin. The unfortunate
prisoners, to the number of between eleven and twelve
hundred, were handed over on Hamilton Moor to the care
of Archibald Cockburn of Langtoune, Colonel of the Berwick-
shire Regiment of Militia, with instructions to escort them
to Edinburgh and to hand them over on arrival to the
Magistrates, who " have undertaken to secure them with

[1] *Council Records*, xxviii. 133.   [2] *Ibid.* xxix. 130.

the Town Guards."[1] After a weary journey, the unfortunates reached the city on 24th June, and were incarcerated by order of the Privy Council in the "Inner Greyfriars' Yard"—the grass yard of between two and three acres previously referred to. The instructions as to their custody were severe. The sentries were to be personally responsible for the safety of their prisoners, and were to answer, by a throw of the dice, "Body for Body for the Fugitives without any exception," while the officers were to answer for the sentries, and the town for the officers. None of the citizens were to be permitted to approach the Greyfriars' Yard except those who brought charitable gifts of meat and drink. The daily food supplied by order of the priest-ridden Privy Council consisted only of *one penny loaf to each prisoner*, the City Fathers contributing nothing. The only analogous entry noted in the City Records is that of 10th September— "to furnish coall and candle for the guaird that attends the prisoners in the Grayfrier Yeard; and doe approve of the Inbringing of the Watter to the said prisoners." The Magistrates, therefore, on the approach of the cold weather, made due provision for the comfort of the military guard, and only at that date provided, by means of a pipe, a proper supply of water to their unfortunate prisoners. The detailed *Army Accounts* also prove that, on 1st July, there were no fewer than 1184 prisoners in " ye Greyfreirs and Heriot's Hospitall." It is evident, although the records of that institution furnish no information, that the wounded were taken to the Hospital, where they received attention at the hands of surgeons sent by the Magistrates. On the 29th June, Lauderdale sent authority for the trial of the prisoners, "and that you put them to the torture if they refuse to inform in what you have pregnant presumptions to believe they know. When this is done, We do, in the

---

[1] For details and authorities, see article on "The Covenanters' Prison," by the present writer, in *The Book of the Old Edinburgh Club*, ii. p. 81.

P

next place, *approve the motion made by you* of sending three or four hundred of these prisoners to the Plantations, for which We authorise you to grant a warrant in order to their Transportation." It is apparent that the proposal to banish several hundreds of the unfortunates as white slaves to the Plantations—if not also to make use of torture—originated in a suggestion by the Privy Council in Edinburgh, of which the Bishop of Edinburgh was the most active member.

Under the pacific influence of the Duke of Monmouth, the Privy Council issued an order on 4th July, offering to liberate the majority of the prisoners upon their signing a bond undertaking not to again take up arms against the King. Several hundreds of the prisoners took advantage of the provisions of this Act, and within a week thereafter their number, as shown in the Accounts, fell to a total of 338, although, by the arrival of other prisoners from Stirling, Linlithgow, and Glasgow, the number by the 16th had increased to 380. In the beginning of the month of August, there were *only* 280 prisoners detained in the Inner Greyfriars' Yard. On the morning of the 14th what was termed a gracious Act of Indemnity by King Charles—*but dated on 27th July*—discharging all, with the exception of the ministers, heritors, and ringleaders, who had taken part in the rebellion, was proclaimed with great pomp and ceremony at the Cross of Edinburgh. In the afternoon, the two unfortunates, John Kid—who had been imprisoned in the Greyfriars, and had suffered the barbarous torture of the " boots "—and John King, were publicly executed; and, in the evening, the Magistrates celebrated the granting of the Act of Indemnity by the lighting of bonfires in the streets. The studied dramatic arrangement of the occurrences on this day—the awful tragedy of the executions carefully sandwiched between the (delayed) proclamation and the public rejoicings in the evening—has naturally been the subject of much unfavourable comment ; and one is lost in wonder at the pitiful spirit that animated the members of the Privy Council and their Episcopal adherents on this occasion.

In this month of August a third movement, expressly intended as an act of vengeance for the murder of Archbishop Sharp, began to develop. It was evidently inspired from ecclesiastical sources, and first appears in a letter dated 26th July from the King, in which he commands that criminal proceeding be taken against nine of the prisoners who had taken part in the rebellion, " with this additional consideration of having *owned these murderers*." The instructions in the letter are to the effect that these nine men are to be executed " merely upon that account," and that, on conviction, they " are to be hanged in chains upon the Place where the horrid Murder was committed." Now, it was well known to the members of the Privy Council that a large number of the prisoners held the opinion that the rising was not a rebellion, and that the slaughter of the Archbishop was simply an act of retribution—not a murder ; and it was from among these, who had no connection with the crime, that the nine victims were to be selected.   On the 15th, a list of thirty names was sent up to London, out of which twenty-one were selected for trial.   In the meantime, many of the ministers in Edinburgh urged the poor creatures to sign the Bond and thereby obtain their liberty ; while another and extreme section as stoutly maintained that it was *sinful* to do so. A batch of fifteen of the recusants were then marched down to the Tolbooth, and on the 20th of August their numbers became thereby reduced to 240. On the 22nd the following nine specially selected men were " Indyted and accused for the crymes of treason and Rebellion in June last, in joyning with the Rebells at Bothwellbridge, and continueing in rebellion with them till they were defate " :—

William Retchardson in Stenhouse,
Thomas Brown, Shoemaker in Edinburgh,
James Balfour in Gilstoun,
Alexander Balfour, Tennent there,
Thomas Williamson in Over Waristoun,
Robert M'Gill, Wobster in Gallosheills,
Robert Miller in Watterfoot,
James Paton in Inverkeithing,
Andrew Thomson in Sauchie.

These men were charged before the Lords of Justiciary as the " cheiff officars," or leaders, " because they hade in ane oppin assemblie declaired (uplifting ther hands) that these heads had murdered the Arch Bishop of St. Andrews, and did by these ther officers condemne and execut those who had served his majestie and parliament." The trial was delayed from time to time until the 10th November, when thirty-three, including the nine above recited, of the prisoners in the Tolbooth, the majority of whom had been transferred thither from the Greyfriars, were brought before the Justiciary Court. All these had repeatedly refused to accept the terms offered—as the indictment states, " by another unparalleled instance of His Majestie's unwearied goodness "— not to take up arms again. Of this number, six were committed for trial—" Andrew Sword in Galloway, Thomas Brown in Edinburgh, James Wood in Aire, John Weddall in Llidesdale, David Hardie in Fyff, and John Cleyd in Kilbryd." Their own declarations, or " confessions " as they were termed, in which they admitted having been captured in arms and refused to subscribe the Bond of Indemnity, were used against them by Sir George Mackenzie, the Lord Advocate—" Bloody Mackenzie "—as the only adminicle of proof. Of the six, only one—David Hardie—was acquitted, the other five being sentenced to be " caryed to the muir of Magus within the Sherriffdome of Fyff, and that place thereof wher his Grace the late Archbishop of St. Andrews wer murdered, upon Tuesday the eighteint day of November instant betwixt two and four o'clock in the efternoon, and ther to be hanged on ane gibbet till they be dead, and ther bodies to be hung up on chaines in the said place till they rott, and all ther lands, heretages, goods, and gear to be forfault and escheat to our soveraigne Lord's use for the treasonable crymes above specified; which wer pronounced for doom." It need hardly be pointed out that none of these five victims of ecclesiastical vengeance had any share, directly or indirectly, in the murder of the Archbishop. They bravely met their fate, and a memorial stone now marks the place of their martyrdom.

On the 15th of November the whole of the prisoners left in the Greyfriars, to the number of 210, were marched down under a military escort to Leith, whence they were put aboard the sailing vessel called the *Crown*. Here other brethren in affliction from the Tolbooths of Edinburgh and the Canongate were also collected, raising the total number to 257, intended for banishment to Virginia. The vessel, with its living cargo, sailed from Leith Roads on 27th November; but of the story of its short and disastrous voyage, no contemporary account seems to exist. In the year 1679 there were no newspapers published in Scotland. The particulars, however, can be gleaned from a number of works written by sympathisers shortly after the event. From the first the weather proved unfavourable, and, ultimately, on 10th December, the ship was driven on the rocks by the violence of the storm, and became a total wreck. The scene of the disaster has been identified as a place called Scarvating, on the western side of the Moul Head of Deerness, and of the wretched prisoners over two hundred were drowned. A list of the names of these unfortunate victims of " man's inhumanity to man," so far as could be identified, is to be found in the first edition of the *Cloud of Witnesses*, published in 1714. A plain stone monument has been erected within recent years on a site overlooking the scene of the disaster.

In the following year the learned Gilbert Rule, who afterwards became minister of Greyfriars, felt the heavy hand of the Episcopalian Inquisition for having dared to baptize two children in St. Giles, where he had preached at the request of the minister. For this heinous offence he was brought before the Privy Council on the 8th of April, and the record is now quoted as showing the spirit that animated the dominant clerical faction of the day. In the *Decreta* of the Register of the Privy Council it is stated that he—

"Upon the first of April instant, did take upon him to hold and keep a conventicle within the Old Kirk of Edinburgh called St. Geilles Church, at which he did preach, expound scripture, and pray, and did baptize severall children, and, particularly, a child of John Kennedy's, Apothecary, and another of James Livingston's, Merchant in Edinburgh, at which conventicle the saids two persons presented and had their children baptized."

The Privy Council, therefore—

"Doe find the said Mr. Gilbert Rule, Defender, by his oune confession, guilty of keeping a conventicle and disorderly baptizeing of two children in St. Geilles Kirk in Edinburgh, and, therefor, suspends him from the benefits of his Majestie's indulgence for preaching in the Paroch of Prestounhaugh, and appoints him to be sent to and keepet prisoner in the Isle of Basse till the King's Majestie's pleasure be known anent him, and gives Order and Warrand to Generall Dalzell to send him prisoner to the said Isle by such a guard as he shall think fit, and, until he be sent away, that he be keept prisoner in the tolbooth of Edinburgh."

The fathers of the two children were fined, one in the sum of £100 and the other in £200 Scots. Rule remained only a few weeks on the Bass Rock when he fell dangerously ill of a violent attack of ague, and was released for a time, on finding caution to the amount of 10,000 merks, provided he remained within a radius of half a mile of the city.   In a confirmatory letter from King Charles, approval is expressed of the Privy Council's action in sending Rule a prisoner to the Bass " for his insolent usurping a pulpit in Our City of Edinburgh."   The letter also furnishes instructions " to mantaine and inviolatly preserve the sacred Order of Episcopacy."   Among the instructions appear—

" 7th, you are carefully to put in execution your Acts for removing the familyes of irregular Outed Ministers out of the Cittyes of Edinburgh, St. Andrews, and Glasgow, these being usually the resorts of disaffected persons, and the secret nurseries of schisms and trouble ";

and under the 8th section, non-conformist preachers are forbidden to preach either in the city or within a radius of twelve miles thereof.   The reason for this extension of the limit to twelve miles was that, under the former limit of two miles, " the citizens and others flock out in multitudes to those irregular meetings."   On his return to the Bass, Rule again fell ill, and on a further petition to the Council, he was banished the kingdom, under a Bond of 5000 merks, never to return.   During the early winter of 1681, the parishioners living in the western portion of the parish complained to the Town Council that they were much prejudiced in their attendance at the Church through the want of a bell ; and, on the 23rd of November, the Magistrates appointed that the old bell in the Tron Kirk steeple should be placed in the tower of the Greyfriars.   It was also intended that the tower should be put into a proper state of repair, and that some " decorment " should be placed on the top.   Nothing seems to have been done during the ensuing three years, and, upon the 4th of June 1684,[1] the Council entered into an agreement with Robert Milne, the Royal Master Mason, for the erection of " ane pricket of stone work of verrie handsome figures upon

[1] *Council Records*, xxxi. 26.

the tope of the grayfrier steiple," as well as that of Heriot's Hospital, at a cost of no less than 6000 merks. The Tron bell was only taken down[1] in the course of this year, and erected in the Greyfriars' tower; but the suggested "decorment" failed, on the score of expense, to take practical shape. At a meeting on 20th August, the Council even seemed to have considered the advisability of placing a peal of three bells in the tower. During the following six years payments appear in the Accounts of the sum of £20 annually for the services of a bell-ringer. In 1690 the old bell was ordered to be taken down as " broken and insufficient,"[2] and Meikle, the Dean of the Hammermen, was instructed to recast it and increase its size by two extra hundredweights of metal. Meikle, therefore, founded a new bell, for which, according to his receipt dated 3rd September 1690, he was paid the sum of £440 Scots, along with £1, 8s. for " drink money."[3]

In August 1685 Mr. Alexander Malcolm, who was then minister of the second charge at Greyfriars, was appointed to preach to the unfortunate prisoners confined in the Tolbooth, for which he received, in addition to his stipend, an annual sum of 500 merks.[4] Two years later, on his translation to the South-East Parish, the Council withdrew this extra allowance, and ordered all the ministers of the " six paroch kirks of the cittie to preach upon the Sabboth dayes by turns," without extra payment.

The Council record of 27th August 1686 brings into prominence a new and certainly original method employed by the citizens in " pegging out " their claims to suitable lairs in the graveyard. The Council seem to have recognised that every citizen possessed the right of burial, without fee or charge of any kind, within the graveyard; and there had arisen considerable competition for lairs along the line

---

[1] *Council Records.*
[2] *Ibid.* xxxiii. 146.
[3] Dean of Guild's Accounts.
[4] *Council Records,* xxxi. 193.

of the boundary walls, as eminently suited for the erection of large funereal monuments. Several of such monuments had, no doubt, been already erected ; but, in certain cases, as the Council complain, the parties had simply " whitened and blackened a great part of the walls of the said kirk with *mourning tears*, quhairby these persons may pretend that the ground opposite yairto pertains to them " ! [1] In this way a large portion of the available wall space threatened

to be *ornamented* in this peculiar fashion, and to put an end to the unseemly practice, the City Fathers issued express instructions that " all these paintings upon the kirk walls were to be expunged and obliterat." Permission thereafter to bury in these lairs was only to be granted to parties willing to erect marble monuments upon the graveyard boundary walls. In further implement of these instructions, another Order was issued on 5th August of the following year, that all sepulchral monuments to be

"Bloody Mackenzie's" Tomb.

thenceforth erected should be vaulted ; and there can be no question that these two Acts of Council had considerable influence in the design and style of several of the huge monuments to be seen in the graveyard at the present day. One of the largest is that to the memory of Sir George Mackenzie of Rosehaugh, who, for the ruthless manner in which, as Lord Advocate, he prosecuted the unfortunate Covenanters, earned the inglorious sobriquet

[1] *Council Records*, xxxii. 43.

Q

of " Bloody Mackenzie."   On the other hand, the most pathetic monument in the cemetery is that to the memory of the unfortunate Covenanters who suffered during the Episcopalian ascendancy. The original stone, erected in terms of an Act of Council of 28th August 1706, is now preserved in the Municipal Museum. The site of the monument and its surroundings formed part of the garden of the ancient Grey Friars of Observance, which was turned into the common place of burial for malefactors, within whose ranks the Covenanters were officially placed. Within the church itself there were many tombs, but the largest and most imposing was that erected to the memory of Sir George Lockhart of Lee, Lord President of the Court of Session, who, in revenge for an adverse decision given by him in court, was waylaid and murdered by John Chiesley of Dalry. The foul deed created intense sympathy among all classes; and, before execution, Chiesley underwent the torture of the " boots," the favourite instrument of punishment during the Episcopalian régime. It is probable that this was the last occasion on which this dreadful judicial weapon for extorting confession was brought into use in this country. In giving their sanction, in 1689, to the erection of this monument, the Council declared that Lockhart's death " has been ane inexpressible losse to this kingdome and particularly to this ancient cittie "; but it was not until the year 1719, when a fresh grant was issued to the family,[1] that the memorial was erected at the south-east corner of the church, where the marble bust of Dr. Robert Lee has been recently placed.

Regarding the appointments to the office of grave-digger in the old cemetery, there is evidence in the Minutes of Council of 23rd May 1690, of the wretched system introduced during the Restoration period of exacting royalties on many of the public appointments, however small. In the

[1] *Council Records*, xlvi. 121.

Rev. Dr ROBERT LEE,

Minister of Old Greyfriars (1843-1868).

present instance, George Shearrer was elected to be one of the *grave makers*; and the Council, even in the appointment to such a humble office, imposed on Shearrer the obligation " to pay £20 Scots yearly to John Watsone, late Keeper of the Potterraw and West ports." The Council generously provided, however, that this sum of £20 was to be the sole deduction out of his dues.[1] In other words, the shrewd Town Council transferred from their own shoulders to those of Shearrer, the duty of providing an old age pension of £20 to their old servant, the keeper of the Potterrow and West Ports.

XI

THE REVOLUTION TO THE PRESENT TIME

The landing in England, in 1688, of William of Orange brought in its train a complete and lasting change in the constitution of the country. The theory of government by the Divine right of kings received a rude shock from which it never recovered; and the whole bench of bishops and archbishops, intruded upon the Church of Scotland by the personal acts of the Stuart kings, was swept away. Presbyterianism thereupon regained its former footing as the religion of the country. The main agent in bringing about this transformation was the celebrated William Carstares, who was appointed in 1704 to the Church of the Greyfriars. He was even more distinguished as a states-man than as a divine, and, as a recent writer[2] has remarked, there has seldom been an ecclesiastic of any Church who has taken part in politics with greater honour to himself and

[1] *Council Records*, xxxiii. 130.   [2] Dr. Æneas Mackay, *Dict. of Nat. Biog.*

advantage to his country. When in exile in Holland he
made the acquaintance, at an early period of his life, of
William of Orange, who greatly appreciated his abilities.
In the course of his adventurous career he had, through
his support of Presbyterianism, suffered imprisonment for
several years, and even endured the torture of the " thumb-
kins." After the establishment of Episcopacy in 1662, all the
ministers who refused to conform[1] were expelled from their
churches, and imprisonment or execution became the lot of
many. Unfortunately, after the Revolution and re-establishment of Presbyterianism, the non-conformist ministers
were, in their turn, also deprived of their offices; and, in
this way, several of the Edinburgh clergy were forced to
quit their churches. The test of the year 1662 was the
disowning of the Covenant; while that of 1688–89 was the
taking of the oaths of allegiance to the new King and Queen.
Much has been written regarding the regrettable sufferings
of the outed clergy of this date; but it is to be remembered
that Episcopacy at that time, as at the present day, had
only a small hold on the affections of the community. In
any case, the change in Church government was not followed
by the executions, imprisonments, or infliction of torture
that characterised the preceding period. The forms of
worship as laid down by John Knox, including extempore
prayers, continued down to the Revolution to be those in
regular use in the Episcopalian service. After the experience
of the years 1638 to 1660, the bishops, in view of the strong

---

[1] About 350 were ejected. Their places were filled by men whom Bishop
Burnet thus describes: "The new incumbents were generally very mean, and
despicable in all respects . . . the worst preachers I ever heard, ignorant to
a reproach, and many of them openly vicious. They were a disgrace to their
order and their sacred functions." The ejected Presbyterian ministers were,
he further tells us, "a grave, solemn sort of people. Their spirits were eager
and their tempers sour, but they had an appearance that created respect. They
were related to the chief families of the country, either by blood or marriage,
and had lived in so decent a manner that the gentry paid great respect to them."
(Burnet's *History*, i. 156.)

feeling that existed throughout the country, wisely refrained from making any alteration in the forms of public worship, and this fact is emphasised by Bishop Rattray when describing the forms of worship practised in his own Church, even after the Revolution : " The method in our ordinary Assemblies on the Lord's Day was almost the same with that of the Presbyterians, beginning with singing a stanza or two of the Metre Psalms, after which followed an extemporary Prayer, during which, as well as at singing of the Psalms, most of the Congregation sat irreverently on their breech, only they were uncovered. Then came a long Sermon, the text of which was no sooner read but most of the people put on their hats and bonnets. After the Sermon followed another extemporary Prayer, at the conclusion of which they said the Lord's Prayer, then another stanza or two of the Metre Psalms, which they concluded with a Doxology ; but the people sat likewise during all the time of this last prayer and Psalms, in the same manner as in those before Sermon, only they rose up at the Doxology, tho' some thought even that too superstitious ; whether they generally stood up at the Lord's Prayer, I am not so certain. After the Doxology, the Congregation was dismissed with a Blessing ; but, indeed, most of them didn't wait for it." [1] Bishop Rattray admits that this affinity of the Episcopalian to the Presbyterian form of worship led many to attend the Presbyterian kirks ; " for," he explains, " the Divine right of Episcopacy and the necessity of an Ordination by Bishops for conferring the Sacerdotal Powers, was then very little known among our Laity, perhaps not by several of our Clergy themselves." [2] The natural interpretation of this statement of the worthy Bishop is, that the interpolation of the " Divine right of Episcopacy " in the Presbyterian Church of Scotland had not been a success, either among the laity or even the clergy of his own persuasion.

[1] *Eccles. Chron. for Scotland*, Dr. Gordon, ii. 109.   [2] *Ibid.* 111.

Indeed, it was not until the following century that attempts were made by the Scottish Episcopal Church to assimilate the forms of church worship to those of the Church of England ; and it may be asserted that the alleged " Divine " right of Episcopacy was the direct cause in this country of no fewer than three revolutions, with all their attendant miseries.

That much suffering and hardship became the lot of the outed ministers there can be no question. In 1691 James Hutchison, minister of Greyfriars, was deposed for contumacy, and was forced, six years afterwards, to appeal to the Council for pecuniary assistance. In 1697, and again in 1698, he was granted a donation of 100 merks ; and in February 1699 he received a third gift of 100 merks " on account of his present hard and pinching straits." During the same year he was restored to his position in the ministry, although not reappointed to his old church. Alexander Ramsay was another ex-minister of the Greyfriars who appealed to the Council for assistance, and was paid a gratuity of 200 merks on account of " the petitioner's straits and difficulty by reasone of the hardnes of the tymes." [1] The sufferings of the outed ministers found expression in a pathetic appeal to the Council in 1705, which was given in by two of their number " in name and behalf of the indigent ministers of the episcopal perswasione." The petition pointed out that their ministers " are reduced to great want and necessitie, amidst which they must neids have perished if they had not been supplied by the charitable assistance of good people. The petitioners doe inginously confess that the Magistratts of the good toune and the good neighburis therein have expressed great tenderness and kyndness towards them." [2] It appears that two years had elapsed since any allowance from the municipal treasury had been made ; and the grant by the Council of £200 Scots, during

---

[1] *Council Records*, xxxvi. 26, 17th December 1697.   [2] *Ibid.* xxxviii. 246.

this and each of the two succeeding years, cannot be said to have erred on the side of generosity. The first minister, after the change of government, sent to the Greyfriars was the Gilbert Rule whose experiences on the Bass Rock have just been related. On his return from exile he was elected by the Town Council on 7th December 1688, and in 1690 he was also chosen to fill the important post of Principal of the University of Edinburgh. On the deposition of James Hutchison in 1691, much excitement was created among the kirk-session and congregation on the appointment by the Town Council of Mr. James Wilkie from North Leith to Greyfriars, and, in deference to their wishes, he was ultimately translated to Lady Yester's Church. His name appears in the Greyfriars' Kirk-Session Record as having acted on one occasion as Moderator, and the cause of the apparent antipathy to him is unknown. In terms of a Decree by the Court of Session, the Town Council resolved on 6th January 1692 [1] to send a deputation to the Presbytery of Edinburgh, to demand that all the communion cups and other utensils of the city churches be handed over to them. This was only a precautionary measure in case of their possible removal by any of the now dissenting ministers. The Session Records of 6th January 1701, and subsequent dates, show that the silver communion cups and baptismal basin and laver were then in possession of the Session, and that the cups, two of which were gilt, were encased in separate boxes. These were placed in the custody of one of the elders ; while the silver basin and laver were " putt in Thomas Stewart his hand for dayly use of ye kirk." In the month of February 1692, the Lord Provost proceeded to London, and attempted to regain for the city the revenues of the Bishopric of Orkney, out of which the stipends of the city ministers had been wont to be paid. In his negotiations, his lordship gave the authorities there

---

[1] *Council Records*, xxxiv. 2.

a vivid and interesting picture of the condition of Edinburgh at the time, and of the financial burdens under which the citizens groaned.[1]   John Hamilton, minister of Cramond, received a call to Greyfriars in the course of this year; and the Records tell us that a sum of ten guineas was paid to Lieutenant Gilbert Hall, for his trouble and success "anent the loosing of Mr. John Hamiltoune, one of the present ministers of Edinburgh, out of his charges in Ireland, before the Church judicatories thereof."[2]

During the excitement of the many political changes incidental to the Revolution, little had been done in the way of maintaining the fabric of the old church in proper repair; and the Kirk-Session presented in 1695 a strongly worded petition to the Council, drawing attention, in particular, to the ruinous condition of the church roof. The matter was entrusted to the hands of Patrick Skirving, a plumber, who completed the repairs and entered into an agreement with the Council to maintain the church sufficiently "watertight" for an annual sum of £7, or, in lieu thereof, to provide him yearly with a seat in the kirk.[3] The worthy plumber, who was a member of the congregation, accepted the use of the pew in preference to the money. In the following year the south door was, as previously mentioned, converted into a window; while the east loft and the west loft (which belonged to Heriot's Hospital) were both enlarged.[4] In 1704 the back part of the Heriot loft was ordered to be fitted up to accommodate the poor.[5]

About fifty or sixty years ago, it was the practice to keep an iron collecting-box for the poor at the present entrance from Greyfriars' Place to the churchyard. The custom is an old one, and during the latter half of the seventeenth century and for over one hundred years thereafter, the box was placed at the head of the steps of the burial yet at the

---

[1] *Council Records*, xxxiv. 9.   [2] *Ibid*. xxxv. 42.   [3] *Ibid*. xxxv. 186.
[4] *Ibid*. xxxv. 232, 255.   [5] *Ibid*. xxxviii. 206.

foot of the Candlemaker Row, which in those days was the fashionable entrance. The amount of the collections received at the latter place was considerable, and it was the custom to examine the box at each quarterly communion, and to add the contents to the usual collections in the church, under deduction of ten merks to the beadles. Sums of £49, £76, £102, and £69 are noted as having been found in the box during the year 1700–1. The Kirk-Session, therefore, became the principal charitable organisation of the parish, and in the newly discovered Session Records [1] it will be seen that they regularly maintained a set of pensioners—poor women in particular—whilst, among a variety of claimants for assistance, are to be found Divinity and other students. There were two sets of pensioners who received weekly or quarterly doles, and it was the duty of the elders and their deacons to visit the weekly pensioners living within their respective bounds, and inquire into their special circumstances; while the quarterly pensioners had to appear in person in the aisle of the church. The keeper of the Inner Yard was paid the sum of seven shillings a week for the support of a foundling, who, on reaching school age, would be sent to the Charity School for education. Special collections were also made in the church in cases of calamity occurring within the city. For example, in order to relieve the state of destitution brought about by the great fire in the Lawnmarket in the year 1700, the Kirk-Session collected, within the six bounds of the parish, the sum of £419, out of which 13s. 6d. was lost through "light money," *i.e.* coins not up to standard weight. Eight years later, on the occasion of another conflagration in the Canongate, the Session managed

---

[1] The writer has discovered the existence of one small volume (1732 to 1736) of Session Records in the City Chambers, and another large one (1709 to 1720) in the library at the Assembly Hall. The first volume of the Session Records of the New Greyfriars is also preserved there. All these volumes should be preserved either in the Central Library at the Assembly Hall, or, preferably, in the General Register House.

R

to collect for the sufferers the sum of £240. But the poor
were even more in evidence in these days than they are now,
and, in the year 1698, the Town Council sent a letter to the
General Kirk-Sessions, intimating that " they have now
freed the streets and doors of the citie of the multitude of
beggars, and are at a great charge in maintaining [them] in
the New Grayfrier yard, and are confident that all good
neighbours are so sensible of their being freed of a great
charge and truble thereby, that they will freely contri-
bute." [1]

It will be seen from this that the yard in which the
Covenanting prisoners were interned was now utilised in a
similar way for the poor of the city. An hospital, of some
description, must have been erected about this time, which,
from the year 1703 onwards, became the recognised residence
of the poor.[2] In June 1711, the Session, on the recommenda-
tions of the General Sessions, made a house-to-house collection in the parish on behalf of " the comon beggars which,
by the Magistrats Order are put in ane hospitall for frieing
the neighbourhood of trouble." [3] In the month of August a
sum of £96 was collected for this purpose, and in the following
December another sum of £109 was obtained. The Session
Records further show that the congregation were generous
supporters of this institution. In the year 1703 the western
section of the new Greyfriars' Yard was given off by the Council
to form the southern extension of the old graveyard; and this
small strip of ground has, until recently, been erroneously
identified as that in which the Covenanters were imprisoned.
The stone archway, with its funereal ornaments, and the iron
gate were only placed there in the year 1704—twenty-five
years after the date of the Covenanting incident. On the

---

[1] *MS. Record of General Kirk-Sessions.*

[2] 20th October 1704. Act anent the putting of the begging poor to work
within New Gray freris. *Council Records*, xxxviii. 172.

[3] *Greyfriars' Session Record*, ii. 122.

centre portion a Charity Workhouse was erected, which, during the middle of last century, was disponed by the Parochial Board—the modern representatives of the City Kirk-Sessions and their treasurer—to the Queen's Edinburgh Volunteers to be converted into the present Drill Hall; while on the eastern section, a lunatic asylum for paupers, afterwards known as Bedlam, was erected. It was in this asylum that poor Fergusson, the Edinburgh poet and proto-type of Burns, died. The support which the Council gave to the unfortunate Robert Monteith in compiling his book on the monumental epitaphs in the Greyfriars' burial ground is, perhaps, worthy of notice. On 6th September 1714, the Council appointed two of their number to revise the work, and "cause print the same on the toune's expenss." They also gave him a general protection against its being re-printed or pirated by local printers for a period of twelve years.[1] The Kirk-Session purchased a copy of the book in 1716, at a cost of 36s.

The first three volumes of the Kirk-Session Records prove that the Session, in face of the restrictions of both the Scottish and Imperial Parliaments, continued to investigate and issue sentences imposing pains and penalties on offenders in what they termed cases of discipline. In the event of moral delinquents failing to appear, the Session had no hesitation in ordering the arrest of all their goods and chattels until they " compear in publick to remove the said scandall." Not content with their inquisitorial investiga-tions into the private lives of individuals, it was the duty of these elders and deacons to hunt up and report to the Presbytery all Papists, preachers at meeting-houses, chaplains and " pedigogers " or schoolmasters—presumably of the Roman Catholic persuasion. In 1712 the Session recom-mended that application be made to the Civil Magistrates " for stopeing papists from teaching any science, art, or

[1] *An Theater of Mortality*, R. Monteith, 1704. *Council Records*, xxxviii. 133.

exercise in families, or outwith the same."[1] Even the
children were spied and reported on ; and the Session urged
that those " under popish parents, Tuttors, Curators, and
Governours be taken from them, and application made to
Her Majestie's Advocat and Solicitors for that effect." It
was even proposed to take Lady Greden's children from her,
and place them under the care of certain of her Protestant
relatives.[2] On Sundays the elders scoured the streets, and
when noises were heard these " Searchers of the Street,"[3]
as they were called, entered private dwellings, which they
ransacked in the hope of finding something " censurable."
A minister of Old Greyfriars at a later period has characterised
the system as odious, " with its perpetual petty interference
with almost every action of life ; its intrusions into all affairs ;
its meddling and thrusting its officious counsels and reproofs
into everything ; so that even the sanctity of domestic
life could not escape its inquisitorial impertinence ; so that,
to quote the words of a contemporary observer, ' a nurse
shall not dare to quiet her child but with a psalm, and you
must not presume to ask what o'clock it is, without a text
to prove that the question tends to edification.' "[4] There
was no Jewish Mission in those days, but the appearance in
the city of a Jew named Moses Mosias seems to have excited
hopes in the breasts of the City Fathers of the possibility
of making a proselyte ! He was granted permission " to
merchandize within ye toun and priviledges dureing ye
Councill's pleasure ; and in case he turned Christian,
declares they will admit him Burgess gratis."[5] There was,
evidently, more hope in the conversion of a Jew than of a
Papist—an expectation upon which modern experience casts
considerable doubt !

On 11th September 1704, the Town Council elected Mr.

[1] *Greyfriars' Kirk-Session Record,* ii. 154.
[2] *Ibid.* 155.
[3] *Ibid.* i. 18.
[4] *Life of Dr. Robert Lee,* Principal Story, i. 142.
[5] *Council Records.*

William Carstares, at that time Principal of the University, to be one of the ministers of the " good toune," and, on an intimation for the approval of the Presbytery, " the Lord Provost, in name of the Counsell, gave their thanks to the presbiterie, and thereafter the Counsell placed, fixed, and settled the said Mr. William Carstairs in his Ministerie in the Grayfreir Kirk as colleauge with Mr. James Hart, and appointed him to enter to that charge the second Sabath of November next, and allowed him 2200 merks scotts of yearly sallaraie as principall of the Colledge comencing from Mertimes next." [1] It is remarkable that Carstares, who was the chief promoter of the Union between England and Scotland, should find one of his strongest opponents in his colleague, Mr. Hart. Three years later, on 10th December 1707, Carstares was translated to the New Kirk at St. Giles, much to the regret of his old congregation, who transmitted to the Council an ineffectual petition strongly urging his retention in Greyfriars. The petition was signed by the Kirk-Session and the leading members of the congregation, to the number of 85.[2] A successor to Mr. Carstares was not found until four years after his departure, when Mr. Mathew Wood was translated from the parish of Leslie in Fife to the Greyfriars. Mr. Hart seems to have had an unpleasant experience with his precentor, Daniel Cameron. A girl named Agnes Johnston alleged to the Session that Cameron " both draged, dunsht, and niped her " during the time of public worship. It appears she had dispossessed the precentor's children of their seat, and he urged in his defence that he " only pusht her off the same with his elbow." When brought before the Session, the record tells us that he upbraided the minister by " calling him a byassed person, aleadgeing he spoke bousterously to him and in passion, not lyk a servant of Jesus Christ, but rather like a dragoon." [3]

[1] *Council Records*, xxxviii. 166.   [2] *City Muniments Report*, xvii. 68.
[3] *Greyfriars' Kirk-Session Record*, ii. 145.

For this "impertinient cariage to the Referrend Mr. Hart" the precentor was suspended for three months, and only reponed at Mr. Hart's request. In October 1710, the Session had before it for consideration a long overture from the Presbytery complaining of the flocking of the people to various churches at the communion "upon pretence to hear sermon in ye churchyeard"—a practice which Burns satirised in his poem of the "Holy Fair"; and the Presbytery recommended that, thereafter, communion should only be held twice a year in all the Edinburgh churches.[1]

In addition to the Charity Workhouse, the General Sessions also established a Charity School in the South Greyfriars' Yard. Probably, at this time, one of the rooms in the Hospital was employed for this purpose; but at the end of the eighteenth century a school was erected on a site in the south-east corner of the yard, between the lunatic asylum called Bedlam, and the third city wall. It formed, un-doubtedly, the real original Ragged School of Edinburgh. The school seems to have been under the direct supervision of the Kirk-Session of Old Greyfriars, who sent at stated intervals an elder, accompanied by his deacon, to report on the state of proficiency of the children.[2] The Session seems even to have paid the salary of the schoolmaster, whose name in 1715 was Arthur Couper.[3] The Kirk-Session of the New Greyfriars, at a later period, also took up the question of the support of this school, and at one of their first meetings there is a notice of a sum of £4, 8s. 8d. having been collected by all the members of the Session as a "voluntar collection for the Charity School"; but, in point of fact, both Sessions became deeply interested in its progress. At first the children were boarded out by the General Sessions among certain "honest people"; but, in 1726, orders were issued that

---

[1] *Greyfriars' Kirk-Session Record*, ii. 84, 87.
[2] *Ibid.* ii. 124. [3] *Ibid.* ii. 370.

the children should be lodged only with such persons " that will not detain them from School." [1]

Many of these collections were, of course, made by order of the City Fathers, who found in the churches a convenient means of advertising their municipal charities; and one great feature is, necessarily, the catholicity of the objects on whose behalf contributions were solicited. A collection of £7 is noted as having been contributed " by all the members of the Session for the Church in New York in America"; while others were for the repair of a new harbour at Aberbrothic, and for the building of a bridge across the Dee at Braemar.

In the meantime, the City Fathers had been much exercised regarding the storage of gunpowder, belonging to the gunmakers in the city, and the selection of a common magazine for their use, situated apart from the buildings of the town. They finally resolved upon the clumsy tower of the Greyfriars' Church as a suitable storehouse for such a purpose. On the morning of 7th May 1718, an explosion took place which destroyed both the tower and the bell founded by Meikle in 1691, and seriously injured the western gable of the church itself, as well as several of the adjoining monuments. The best account of the disaster is the graphic and entertaining description furnished by the Session Clerk in the pages of his Minute Book :—

" The Session, takeing to their consideration the late conflagration of the Steiple of their Church, whereby the Fabrick therof is much demolished, and they also considering the Conduct of Divine providence in timeing the same, being so very favourable and remarkable, They agreed that the following account thereof should be recorded in maner underwritten, viz. :—That on Wednsday the Seventh of May instant 1718, about a quarter of ane hour befor Two of the Clock in the morning, the Grayfrier Church Steiple was blown up, which Surprized and allaramed the whole City, more

---

[1] *New Greyfriars' Session Record.*

particularly the Grayfrier Congregation. By which the Grayfrier Church sustained so great damnage, as it was rendered unfitt for the Congregation to assemble therein for publick worship till it be repaired ; So that the members of this Congregation were oblidged to meet, some of them in the Lower Commonhall of the Colledge of Edinburgh, and others in the Chappell of Herriot's Hospitall, Others to go to other Churches of this City. Thus, the Congregation, by reason of this disaster befallen our Church, were scattered. What was the true occasion of the blowing up of the Grayfrier Church Steiple is uncertain ; but the generall conjecture is, that it was occasioned by the Plummers leaveing some Fyre in a hole of the Wall where the Bell hung, where they had been working the Thursday befor, being the First of May 1718, and there being severall Barrells of powder in the third and fourth Storries of the said Steeple belonging to the Good Town and to some Merchants, where the Fyre, working downward till it came to the fourth and third Storries, where the said Powder was, did blow it up, and Rent the Western Gevell of the Church, broke all the glass windows, and turned the Sclates of the Church, and broke a great deall of the Leadden high roof of the Church. Even in that sad and alaraming dispensation, there was much of the Mercy of God both to this City, and to this Congregation in particular, to be observed, and which ought never to be forgot in the comeing of it, that it happened so early in the morning when people were in Bed, and that it did not fall out at such a time of the day when people used to frequent the Churchyeard, or at the hours of Buriall. But, especially, that it did not happen on the Lord's day when the Congregation was mett for publick worship. What havock and desolation would it have made ! Scarce one of the Congregation would have escaped with their life, but wee would have been slain upon the Spott. O what reason have wee to sing of Mercy, that the place of our publick worship, was not made a field of Blood, and that it was not with us, as with these upon whom [the] Tower of Siloam fell. Have wee not then reason to sett up our Ebenezer and say, hitherto the Lord has helped us."

Immediately after the disaster, the Magistrates placed a new magazine at the south-west corner of the middle portion of the *Inner* Greyfriars' Yard ; and, on the erection of the

Principal WILLIAM ROBERTSON, D.D.,

Minister of Old Greyfriars (1761-1793).

Charity Workhouse, they expressly reserved right of access to "their repository for gunpowder built at the south-west corner thereof."[1] This magazine continued in active use until the beginning of the nineteenth century, when it was taken down. The church was repaired in May 1718, when the western gable was rebuilt so as to be in line with the second pillar. The building was thereby considerably reduced in size, although, according to the opinion of the Council, " the kirk thus bounded will be better proportioned than formerly, contain a greater number of hearers, and accommodate them much better." On the 18th of November of the same year, the Town Council agreed to erect a second church at the west end of the old church, and to begin the work in the course of the following spring. The matter was, thereupon, placed in the hands of the architects, and the new church was completed by the 31st December 1722; but it was not until the autumn of the following year that steps were taken for the formation of the new congregation. The two churches, thenceforth, became respectively known as the Old and New Greyfriars. The first meeting, relative to the formation of a congregation and Kirk-Session for the New Greyfriars' Church, was held on the 19th September 1723 in the aisle of the South Kirk of St. Giles. The new parish was formed out of portions taken from the neighbouring parishes of the Tolbooth and Old Greyfriars, and at this meeting there were present the Kirk-Sessions of these two parishes along with a deputation from the Town Council, headed by George Drummond, then Dean of Guild and afterwards the well-known Lord Provost. The Dean produced a letter from the Presbytery intimating the appointment, as minister to the new parish, of Mr. John Hepburn, from Torryburn in Fife; and in terms of the letter the two Sessions proceeded to select six elders and six deacons to form the first New Greyfriars' Kirk-Session. This Session met on

[1] *Council Records*, 1st September 1731.

S

the 18th October ; and the diets of the communion, beginning on Thursday the 24th, were held for the first time, when the collection amounted to over £16, of which a third was bestowed on private charity. In January 1724 the total rental of the seats in the New Greyfriars' Church amounted to the sum of £967 Scots, and the nucleus of a considerable congregation was formed.[1] Among the seat-holders appear the names of Lord Glencorse, Lady Beliss, Lady Hamilton, Hamilton of Dalserf, and Sir James Dalrymple. The Masters and boys of Heriot's Hospital were removed from the Old to the New Greyfriars, and accommodated in the wester and south wing lofts on the west side of the pulpit, while five new seats in the wester loft were allocated for poor people, servants, and strangers. On 12th June of the same year, the Dowager Countess of Rosebery became a seat-holder in Old Greyfriars. Mr. John Hepburn, the minister of the New, was, at the request of the Session, transferred by the Town Council on 7th June 1732 to the Old Greyfriars' Church.[2] He became almoner to His Majesty in 1747, and died two years later. During the twelve years preceding 10th January 1721, when William Millar from Lady Yester's Church was translated to the Old Greyfriars, James Hart, the minister of the first charge, had acted as pastor of the parish without the assistance of any colleague.[3] Hart was succeeded by William Brown, at whose death, in 1736, William Robertson, then minister of Lady Yester's Church, was elected[4] in response to a strong recommendation by the Kirk-Session. He was a man with historical instincts, and collected much material for historical purposes.

The social customs of the first half of the eighteenth century, particularly in the mode of conducting burials in the Greyfriars' Cemetery, are of some interest. It was a

---

[1] *Council Records.*
[2] *Ibid.* liv. 112.
[3] *Ibid.* xlviii. 334.
[4] *Ibid.* lvi. 340, 28th May 1736.

Rev. Dr JOHN ERSKINE,

Minister of Old Greyfriars' (1767-1803).

time when *grand* funerals were fashionable, from the wealthiest to the poorest citizen, and when people believed, with the Chinaman, "that the most important thing in life is to be buried well." The duties of the humble bellman, as transmitter of funeral invitations, had been superseded by a more imposing official termed the " Disperser of Buriall Letters," and intimations for attendance at funerals were now made by letters " dispersed " by this official or his employees. He also possessed the sole right of employing men, clothed in black gowns and capes, to stand with flambeaux and links in their hands in front of the houses of mourning, and of other men—mutes, as they were afterwards called—dressed also in capes and holding batons, to march in front of the hearse. In 1716 the Town Council issued a series of regulations upon the subject, and appointed Collin Haigs, a burgess of the city, as sole " Disperser " for the time being. They also framed the following table of dues to be enacted from the citizens : [1]—

Imprimis, from the first of September to the first of Apryll, each man standing from 5 to 10 a clock at night with flambous . . . . 8s. Scots.

Item, from the 1st Apryll to the 1st September, for each man standing from 8 to 10 a clock at night . . 6s.

Item, for each man holding a Link the tyme foirsd in the winter season . 7s.

Item, in the summer season . . 5s.

Item, for each Letter dispersed within the citie . . . . 6d.

Item, for each Letter dispersed in the suburbs, viz. Canongate, Westport, Potteraw, and Pleasants . . 1s.

Item, for each Letter dispersed in South and North Leiths . . . 1s. 6d.`

[1] *Council Records*, xliii. 159.

The position of " Disperser " was of so important a nature that under his agreement with the Council, he had to advertise his place of business in the *Courant* newspaper, and to place over it a suitable signboard. In course of time several additions were made to the number of dispersers, who, however, found some difficulty in keeping out others, " yea even the street cadies," from attempting to act as linkmen, or baton men, and in their complaints to the Council the dispersers allege that these outsiders " do take their bread from them." In 1747 four men claimed to have the sole right of dispersing burial letters; but of the four, the Council refused to reappoint one, William Hart, on the score of age, and elected George Robertson, one of the beadles of the New Greyfriars, in his place. It was an age when the tide of prosperity had not yet reached this country, and plurality of offices, however small, was not permitted. Robertson, therefore, resigned his beadleship, and the four were then taken bound to pay over to William Hart the sum of " £30 Scots yearlie for life as aliment out of the first and readiest of their fees." This is another example of the mode then prevalent of providing old age pensions for decayed officials.

The two most distinguished ministers of the Old Greyfriars' Church in the eighteenth century were, undoubtedly, Principal William Robertson, elected in 1761, and Dr. John Erskine, who was appointed six years later. Principal Robertson was a son of the above-named William Robertson, at whose death he was in the enjoyment of a fruitful benefice of about £60 a year at Gladsmuir. The death of his mother within a few days of that of her husband threw upon the young minister's shoulders the whole care of the family, a duty which he nobly performed. Two years later he received from the Town Council payment of the arrears of his father's stipend, as well as of his mother's annat [1]—an allowance

[1] *Council Records*, lxvi. 294.

Rev. Dr JAMES FINLAYSON,

Minister of Old Greyfriars' Church (1793-1799).

Professor of Logic, University of Edinburgh.

of half a year's stipend granted to ministers' widows. In 1762 he was elected Principal of the University, and became Moderator of the General Assembly in the following year. He was a distinguished litterateur, and the greatest historian of his day. As such he was appointed the first Royal Historiographer for Scotland, for which he received the salary of £200 sterling, a sum which is still paid to the occupant of that office. Robertson was a brilliant speaker, and exercised a commanding influence over the general management of the whole Church. The great dispute of the day raged round the question of patronage, which found its greatest supporter in the Principal, while his stoutest opponent was his colleague, the famous Dr. John Erskine. Thus both ministers of Old Greyfriars differed on the subject which, in 1843, had the unhappy effect of rending the Church in twain. Dr. Erskine's father was the author of the well-known *Institutes of the Law of Scotland*, and he himself was a renowned classical scholar. He represented the evangelical side of the Church, and, in his sermons, was famous as a brilliant exponent of Scripture. He was a man of a pious and generous nature, and easily imposed upon by a tale of distress. Both Principal Robertson and Dr. Erskine appear in the pages of Sir Walter Scott's novels. In *Guy Mannering* the Colonel is conducted " to the Greyfriars to hear our historian of Scotland, of the Continent, and of America, preach," while Erskine is described as one of the most distinguished clergymen of the time : " The colleague of Dr. Robertson ascended the pulpit. His external appearance was not prepossessing. A remarkably fair complexion, strangely contrasted with a black wig without a grain of powder ; a narrow chest and a stooping posture ; hands which, placed like props on either side of the pulpit, seemed necessary rather to support the person than to assist the gesticulation of the preacher,—no gown, not even that of Geneva, a tumbled band, and a gesture which seemed scarce voluntary, were the first circumstances which struck a stranger. 'The preacher seems a very ungainly person,' whispered Mannering to his new friend.

" 'Never fear; he's the son of an excellent Scottish lawyer—he'll show blood, I'll warrant him.'

" The learned counsellor predicted truly. A lecture was delivered, fraught with new, striking, and entertaining views of Scripture history—a sermon in which the Calvinism of the Kirk of Scotland was ably supported, yet made the basis of a sound system of practical morals, which should neither shelter the sinner under the cloak of speculative faith or of peculiarity of opinion, nor leave him loose to the waves of unbelief and schism. Something there was of an antiquated turn of argument and metaphor, but it only served to give zest and peculiarity to the style of elocution. The sermon was not read—a scrap of paper containing the heads of the discourse was occasionally referred to, and the enunciation, which at first seemed imperfect and embar-

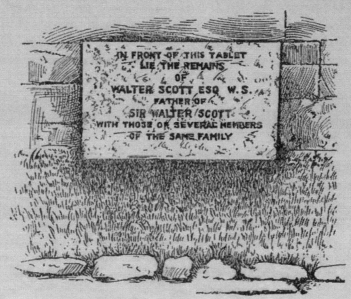

Rev. Dr JOHN INGLIS,

Minister of Old Greyfriars Church (1799-1834).

rassed, became, as the preacher warmed in his progress, animated and distinct; and although the discourse could not be quoted as a correct specimen of pulpit eloquence, yet Mannering had seldom heard so much learning, metaphysical acuteness, and energy of argument, brought into the service of Christianity.

" ' Such,' he said, going out of the church, ' must have been the preachers to whose unfearing minds, and acute, though sometimes rudely exercised talents, we owe the Reformation.' "

Scott, from his youth to manhood, was a constant sitter in Old Greyfriars, and his parents, says an old tutor of the family, " every Sabbath, when well and at home, attended with their fine young family of children and their domestic servants—a sight so amicable and exemplary as often to excite in my breast a glow of heartfelt satisfaction." It was on leaving Greyfriars' Church one Sunday morning that Scott experienced his single romance in real life. Rain had begun to fall, and, with his usual courtesy, he proffered to a young lady of good family and one of the congregation, the use of his umbrella. His offer was accepted, and he escorted the lady to her home, which turned out to be not far distant from his own. Thereafter it became a practice with the young couple to accompany each other to church, and it was soon apparent that Scott had fallen deeply in love with his new acquaintance. Her subsequent marriage, to a gentleman moving in her own circle, put an end to his dream; but years afterwards, when misfortune had overtaken the great novelist, the husband acted the part of a most generous friend to his early rival.

Principal Robertson died in 1793, and was succeeded in the first charge by James Finlayson, who also became Professor of Logic in the University. On his translation to the High Church six years afterwards, Mr. John Inglis from Tibbermore was appointed minister. Inglis, in 1841, received the degree of D.D. from the Edinburgh University, and was elected the following year to be Moderator of the General Assembly. He was a man of some personality, although he did not reach the highest flights in his vocation, and probably he will live in history more as the father of John Inglis, Lord President of the Court of Session, and the greatest " lawyers' Judge " that Scotland has seen, than as minister of the Greyfriars. It was to his efforts, however, that the mission of the Church among the natives of India has proved such a success. There is a story related of this worthy doctor which shows that, like a later minister of Greyfriars, he was conscious of the defects which time had imposed upon our Presbyterian forms of worship. On the occasion of the visit of George IV. to Edinburgh, His Majesty attended Divine service in St. Giles on 25th August 1822. The preacher was Dr. Lamont, then Moderator of the General Assembly, and on his way to church he was overtaken by Dr. Inglis, who suggested that His Majesty, being accustomed to the ritual of the Church of England, would naturally expect to hear the Lord's Prayer recited. Dr. Lamont was very doubtful of being able to repeat it in public correctly—it was his first attempt—and the two divines thereupon stepped aside into a neighbouring close, where Dr. Inglis did not leave his friend until, after repeated rehearsal, he felt sure he could say the prayer properly.[1] The next minister of note in Old Greyfriars was Thomas Guthrie, who was translated thither from the small parish of Arbirlot. He became famous as a preacher, a philanthropist, and a temperance reformer, and it was through his efforts that a Ragged School was formed for the maintenance and education of the poor outcast children of the city. A new Parish Church, called St. John's, was erected by the Council in Victoria Street, and to this

[1] *St. Giles'*, Cameron Lees, 259, note.

Rev. Dr THOMAS GUTHRIE,

Minister of Old Greyfriars' Church (1837-1841).

church, in 1841, Mr. Guthrie, as a minister of the second charge of Greyfriars, was translated. In this way Greyfriars became a single charge, the minister being John Sym, who was elected in 1834. Mr. Sym has been described as " sage in counsel, unselfish in aim, unambitious of power ; a shrewd but amiable judge of human character and conduct, he was ready for every emergency." In short, he was a kindly, amiable gentleman, much beloved by his congregation, many of whom followed him when he joined the secession of the Free Church in 1843. All his elders, however, stuck to the old Church. In the contemporary Minute Book it is stated that " the Reverend John Sym, having become a party to the document referred to in the foregoing deliverance [by the General Assembly declaring the charge vacant], and consequently having thus disqualified himself from being any longer minister of Old Greyfriars' Parish, the church was declared vacant in the usual manner, and intimation thereof given to the Lord Provost, Magistrates, and Town Council of Edinburgh, the patrons." Upon the demission of Mr. Sym, the Reverend Robert Lee, from the parish of Campsie, was unanimously recommended by the Town Council, and appointed minister of Old Greyfriars on 22nd August 1843. His religious views, on his first appearance in the pulpit, were largely evangelical, but before he was able to get into touch with his people the second great disaster to the church occurred. Through the overheating of one of the flues the building took fire on the morning of Sunday, 19th January 1845, and in a few hours nothing was left but the strong old rubble walls of the building. A temporary home had to be found, and by arrangement with the Kirk-Session of the Tolbooth Parish, the Assembly Hall was opened on the Sunday afternoons for the use of the " outed " congregation and its minister. We may here mention that heating apparatus was, for the first time, introduced into the

T

Old Greyfriars' Church, before the Fire of 1845 (Wilson's *Memorials*).

city churches in the year 1809, when the shrewd Town Council exacted, for the purpose of covering insurance, an extra charge of sixpence per seat, or, as described in the Record, " upon each bottom-room of five shillings yearly rent and upwards." [1] Strong pressure was brought to bear upon the Magistrates with a view to expediting the restoration of the church ; but the times were unfavourable. The majority of the Council belonged to the newly formed Free Church of Scotland, and they found pleasure in obstructing and impeding, in every possible way, the repair of the old church. It was not until the year 1857 that the building was completed and opened for public worship. During the interval Dr. Lee found time to consider the contemporary condition of the Church at large, particularly in view of the inroads of Episcopacy among the upper classes. His views and researches brought into prominence the neglected condition of the mode of conducting public worship, as compared with the system in existence prior to the year 1638, which had John Knox for its deviser. While, therefore, taking part in the current discussions of the Presbytery, etc., he refrained from carrying out any of his reforming ideas until he could obtain free occupation of his own pulpit. Although nothing could be done to improve the external appearance of the old rubble walls of the church, the interior was repaired and fitted up by Mr. Cousins, the City Architect, in a graceful, though simple, manner, and all the windows were filled in with painted glass—then a novelty in Presbyterian churches. The great east window was the gift of the congregation, at a cost of three hundred pounds ; while other windows have been placed in memory of Principal Robertson, Dr. Erskine, Dr. Inglis, Mr. Robert Trail, and Dr. Anderson, all ministers of Old Greyfriars. Another window, in memory of George Buchanan, was erected by the late Mr. James Buchanan, a member of the congregation, whose generosity the Town

[1] *Council Records*, cclxiii. 4.

Council recognised by granting him the liferent use of a pew within the church.   On his death the grant was continued to his widow, who resigned the privilege in 1876.   Mr. Buchanan also defrayed the expense of the fitting up of the present vestry with its staircase, while the whole cost of the restoration, as provided by the Town Council, amounted to the sum of £2440, 12s. 7d.[1]

On the return of the congregation to their old church, Dr. Lee began to carry into effect his long-cherished plans for the improvement of the worship.   As already pointed out, both praise and prayer had come to occupy a minor position in the service, and it was towards an improvement of these two important branches that Dr. Lee drew the attention of his flock.   He advised, as a mere matter of propriety, that the congregation should stand during praise, and assume a kneeling posture at prayer; and, with the view of enabling the members to take part in the service, he prepared and printed a volume of Prayers for Public Worship.   By this time, the opposition of the " use and wont " section of the clergy had been strongly aroused, and the matter came before the General Assembly, which, on 24th May 1859, practically sustained the legality of standing at singing and kneeling at prayer.   It declared, however, that the reading of prayer from a book was " an innovation upon and contrary to the laws and usages of the Church in the celebration of public worship ; and the Assembly enjoined Dr. Lee to discontinue the use of the book in question in the services of his church, and to conform in offering up prayer to the present ordinary practice of the Church."   Considering the decision as a large instalment towards victory, Dr. Lee accepted the position, although the prayers continued to be repeated by him from memory, while the congregation made use of the book.   Of course the assertion that read

[1] *Council Records*, cclxxii. 143.

Rev. Dr ROBERT WALLACE,

Minister of Old Greyfriars' Church (1868-1876).

prayers were contrary to the law of the Church was untrue. The Assemblies of 1863 and 1864 gave certain expositions pointing to a relaxation of the unlawful restrictions of 1859, and in 1863 Dr. Lee began, once more, to read from a new edition of his Prayer Book, and thereby again aroused the bigotry of his opponents. An organ had by this time been fitted up in Greyfriars, and, of itself, was the means of rekindling the animosity of his persecutors. It was the first occasion that an organ had made its appearance in any Presbyterian church in this country. Finally, he was arraigned before the Assembly of 1868; but on the day preceding the trial, while returning from a visit to Lord Dunfermline at Colinton, he was struck with paralysis, and fell from his horse at the west end of Princes Street. He only survived a few months, as he died on 12th March 1869. His death created intense sympathy among all classes, and was undoubtedly the means of giving permanence to the reformations in public worship, to obtain which he had sacrificed his life. These reformations have now spread into all the sections of the Presbyterian body, and they have been the means of enabling the Church to regain its former position as the National Zion.[1]

As already mentioned, the knowledge of sacred music in the Church had been well developed down to the year 1640. It may be surmised with some degree of historic truth that, personally, John Knox had no love for music—he was probably " timmer-tuned," to use a Scotticism—but he left the musical portion of the service entirely to the discretion of the respective congregations. Subsequent to 1640, and particularly after the introduction of the English Psalm Book of 1650, there was a distinct falling off everywhere in musical taste and ability; and the position will perhaps be best appreciated from the contents of a Petition addressed by the Old Greyfriars' Kirk-Session to the Town Council in 1804,

[1] Cf. *Life and Remains of Robert Lee, D.D.*, by Principal Story.

urging the appointment of Mr. Alexander Macdonald as Precentor: "In point of character, voice, manner, appearance, and knowledge of music, there is not another so fit for the office, and the attendance of both the Merchant and Trades Maiden Hospitals in our church renders it a matter of peculiar difficulty to conduct the music. Under the charge of an unskilled Precentor, it has often been attended even with such publick indecency, as has been matter of much offence to the most respectable part of the congregation." [1] The difficulties attached to the office of precentor in pre-organ days can be easily imagined, and the impossibility of any one man attempting successfully to pull the singing together by sheer force of lung power, readily understood. In his attempt to restore the musical service to its pristine vigour, Dr. Lee was singularly fortunate in having as his adviser a musical expert in the person of Mr. Joseph Geoghegan, who, on the return of the congregation to Greyfriars, became its first choirmaster. In preparing his Book for Public Worship, Dr. Lee left the selection of the appropriate tunes entirely in the hands of Mr. Geoghegan, the theory being that every psalm in the book should always be sung to the tune so selected. Mr. Geoghegan was a musical enthusiast, and possessed a counter-tenor voice of peculiar sweetness and range. Over his choir and pupils he exercised a strong influence, and through his instrumentality the Old Greyfriars soon became the leading choir in the city. He also introduced numerous anthems, from various sources, as eminently suitable for use in the Presbyterian service. Mr. Geoghegan retired in 1883, and was succeeded in his office by Mr. Peter Glencorse, who, happily for the church, has continued to carry on, with great success, the work of reform in the musical portion of the service.

During the ten years' conflict for reformation in the mode of conducting public worship, Dr. Lee had received

[1] *MS. Report on City Muniments*, vi. 111.

Mr JOSEPH GEOGHEGAN,

Choir Master, Old Greyfriars.

powerful assistance from the intellectual leaders of the Church, including Principal Tulloch, Dr. Norman MacLeod, Dr. Bisset, Mr. Cunningham of Crieff—afterwards Principal Cunningham — and in particular, Dr. Robert Wallace, minister of Trinity College. Dr. Wallace was, perhaps, more closely associated with Dr. Lee than any of the other leaders, and he naturally became his successor in the pulpit of Old Greyfriars. Dr. Lee had intended, after completing the question of reformation in the forms of worship, to take up the more difficult subject of *doctrine*, which, through his unexpected death, became a legacy to his successor.

Dr. Wallace began to enter into the subject of the Higher Criticism, and raised thereby against himself a strong spirit of ill-feeling among the elder portion of the clerical community, in which the managers of a moribund Free Church newspaper joined. Their reporters published his weekly sermons, with long editorial comments on what they termed his theological infirmities, and life was made a burden to him in many ways. He was a man of undoubted ability, and a keen and fearless debater ; but he made one great mistake in the conduct of his life. In 1876 he not only resigned his offices as minister in Old Greyfriars and as Professor of Church History in the University, but he demitted Holy Orders, and gave up using the degree of Doctor of Divinity conferred upon him by the University of Glasgow. Quitting clerical life entirely, he succeeded the well-known Mr. Alexander Russel as editor of the *Scotsman* newspaper. Thenceforth, until his death, which happened twenty-three years afterwards, he led a varied and perhaps not too happy life. After four years spent in the editorial chair, he studied for the English bar, to which he was called in 1883. He was thrice elected Member of Parliament for East Edinburgh, and died on 6th June 1899. He was a clergyman both from choice and training, and had he retained his position as minister of Old Greyfriars, he would, in the course of a short time, have easily overcome the petty clerical clique whose annoyances made life intolerable to him.[1]

With the resignation of Dr. Wallace our story naturally closes. His successor, Dr. John Glasse, who is, happily, still with us, resigned his charge in October 1909, after a long ministry of thirty-three years. The present incumbent is the Rev. Alexander Brown Grant, B.D., who was appointed in 1910.

Unchanging though it appears to the eye, the surface of the Greyfriars' Graveyard has, like the Church itself, undergone many alterations. Burial within this cemetery has, fortunately, been prohibited during the last fifty years; but for a period of nearly three centuries it was the place of sepulture for nearly the whole of the citizens of Edinburgh, and the surface has gradually been raised, through the grim accretions of mortality, to the extent of two or three feet above its original level. To write the story of the relics of humanity that have found a last resting-place here, is probably to indite a history of the city itself, if not actually of the whole country. Every shade and degree of society, from the nobleman down to the dweller in the slums, repose, irrespective of class distinction, within this hallowed ground. Much has been done within the last few years, under the improving hand of Mr. M'Hattie, the City Gardener, to beautify and brighten its appearance; but, as the most sacred spot in the city, its proper maintenance forms an imperative legacy on our municipal administration.

[1] Cf. *Robert Wallace : Life and Last Leaves.*

Rev. Dr JOHN GLASSE,

Minister of Old Greyfriars (1877-1909).

MINISTERS OF OLD GREYFRIARS' CHURCH

1. FIRST CHARGE

1598–1599.	Robert Rollock.	1688–1701.	Gilbert Rule.
1599–16—(?).	Peter Hewat.	1702–1729.	James Hart.
16—(?).	Andrew Ramsay; re-appointed 1620, and again in 1625 to 1641.	1730–1736.	William Brown.
		1736–1745.	William Robertson.
		1747–1760.	James Stevenson.
1641–1647.	George Gillespie.	1761–1793.	William Robertson.
1649–1660.	Robert Trail.	1793–1799.	James Finlayson.
1662.	Robert Douglas.	1799–1834.	John Inglis.
1662–1688.	John Robertson.	1834–1843.	John Sym.

2. SECOND CHARGE

1598–1599.	Peter Hewat.	1687–1691.	James Hutchison.
1620–1622.	Patrick Sandis.	1693–1702.	John Hamilton.
1622–1623.	Robert Boyd.	1704–1707.	William Carstares.
1626.	John Duncanson.[1]	1711–1714.	Mathew Wood.
1630–1637.	James Fairlie.	1721–1732.	William Millar.
1644–1660.	Mungo Law.	1732–1749.	John Hepburn.
1664–1669.	David Stirling.	1750–1754.	Robert Hamilton.
1669–1672.	Alexander Ramsay.	1754–1766.	George Kay.
1672–1674.	Alexander Irving.	1767–1803.	John Erskine.
1674–1681.	Alexander Ramsay.	1804–1837.	Robert Anderson.
1681–1687.	Alexander Malcolm.	1837–1841.	Thomas Guthrie.

3. UNCOLLEGIATE

1843–1868.	Robert Lee.	1877–1909.	John Glasse.
1868–1876.	Robert Wallace.	1910–	Alexander Brown Grant.

[1] Alexander Thomson entered *per incuriam* in *Fasti*.

U

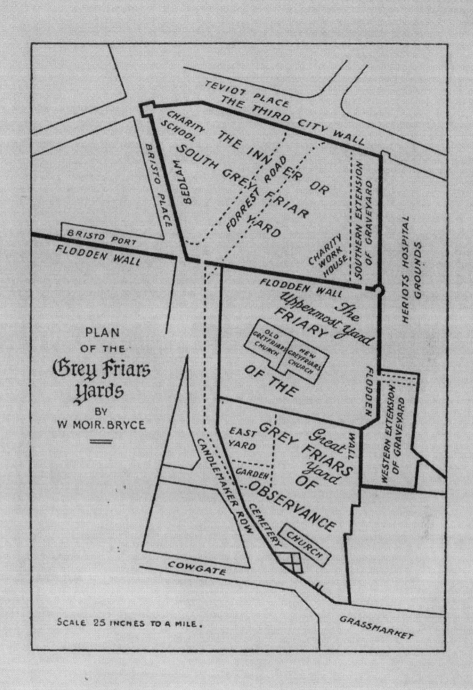

PLAN
OF THE
Grey Friars
Yards
BY
W. MOIR. BRYCE

SCALE 25 INCHES TO A MILE.

Rev. A. B. GRANT, B.D.,

Present Incumbent of Old Greyfriars.

Photo by Moffatt, Edinburgh.

INDEX

———◆———

TOKENS, OLD GREYFRIARS' CHURCH.

FOUNTAIN IN MEMORY OF GREYFRIARS' BOBBY.
Erected by the Baroness Burdett-Coutts.

Printed by MORRISON & GIBB LIMITED, *Edinburgh*

Printed in Great Britain
by Amazon.co.uk, Ltd.,
Marston Gate.